Contents

Major Ernest Read Cooper

Preface

This book was originally published in 1937 by Heath Cranton Ltd., who also produced the original editions of E.R. Cooper's other books, *Mardles from Suffolk* and *A Suffolk Coast Garland*. Many copies of the book were lost when the publishers' premises in Fleet Street were destroyed in the London Blitz, and those that had already been sold are now keenly sought in second-hand bookshops by collectors of Suffolk books.

It was in 1993 that the author's daughter, Miss Judith Cooper, expressed a wish that *Storm Warriors of the Suffolk Coast* should be reissued, but for various reasons the new edition did not appear at that time. The present edition is not identical with the original but has been brought up to date with research by members of the Port of Lowestoft Research Society and others which has thrown new light on the early history of Suffolk's lifeboat service.

It also differs from the original in being illustrated, partly by photographs taken by the author and made available by Miss Cooper. Other illustrations have been provided by Captain John Cragie, great-grandson of the coxswain who is one of the subjects of chapter two, who with his wife Doreen has also provided a great deal of help in the production of the new edition.

Unhappily, because of the time taken to produce this new edition, Miss Cooper did not live to see it published. The editor hopes that she would have approved of what he has done. Certainly she would be pleased that royalties from this new edition will go towards a fund for restoring and preserving the former Southwold lifeboat *Alfred Corry*, now housed in a former Cromer lifeboat shed beside the harbour at Southwold, not far from the spot where her father made his pierhead jump into her during the First World War.

Launching the Southwold No 1 lifeboat, as seen from the lifeboat; a photograph taken by E.R. Cooper.

At sea in the Southwold No 1 lifeboat *Alfred Corry*, another photograph by E.R. Cooper.

A seafaring man: the author

MAJOR ERNEST READ COOPER knew the Suffolk coast as well as any man, and better than most. He wrote from experience of the shipping that used that coast and of the men who sailed those waters in storm as well as calm.

He went to sea himself in the Southwold lifeboat, though as honorary secretary his was a shore job, and he also learnt his way about the channels of the East Coast in his yachts *Spartan* and *Scandal*. The latter was named after Edward FitzGerald's schooner yacht, built by the Harvey shipyard at Wivenhoe on the Colne in 1863 and, according to "Old Fitz", called after "the staple product of Woodbridge".

Cooper's *Scandal* was also Colne-built, by the Brightlingsea yard of Aldous in 1929. A four-tonner with a centreboard and a Stuart Turner auxiliary engine, she replaced the *Spartan* in the early thirties when that old-timer, which had been acquired by Cooper about 1922, became worn out. The *Spartan* had also come from the Colne, from the Wivenhoe yard of J.E. Wilkins, who had built fishing smacks for the Yarmouth fishing fleet. Launched in 1886, she had been designed by G.L. Watson, the well-known Glasgow yacht and lifeboat designer, for a Suffolk owner, W.A.S. Wynne, of Herringfleet.

E.R. Cooper was born not very far from the sea, at Hinton Lodge, Blythburgh, in January, 1865, and at the age of four moved with his parents to Blythburgh Lodge, where he grew up amid the activities of a busy farmhouse. It has been said that he inherited his love of the sea from his maternal ancestors, the Barbers of Hobland Hall, Bradwell, and Great Yarmouth.

His first lifeboat experience was being taken at the age of eight to Dunwich for the christening and launch of the *John Keble* in 1873. He recalled years later that the lifeboat was taken to the church gate for the service and then back to the beach for the launching.

When he left school he was articled to Harry Read Allen, a Southwold solicitor who was also Town Clerk, clerk to the magistrates, and clerk to the Southwold Harbour Commissioners. After his period of training he went to London to seek further experience, but life in a City office was not for him. The severe weather of the winter of 1890-91 undermined his health, and he returned to Suffolk to recuperate. He did not go back to London.

Yet a constitution that was undermined by a London winter seemed proof against the "lazy winds" of the Suffolk coast. In the autumn of 1891 when the brig *Agatha* was ashore at Walberswick E.R. Cooper helped to drag the No 2 lifeboat *Quiver* down to the harbour and launch her; the crew of the brig were, however, rescued by the rocket brigade.

In 1892 he was out again, helping to drag the lifeboat two miles along Easton Cliff to reach the schooner *Elizabeth Kilner*, which was unable to get off a lee shore. Eventually the schooner ran aground in a tremendous sea, near enough to the shore for the crew to be hauled ashore on lines. His sketch of this rescue appeared in the *Daily Graphic* at the time, and was afterwards used to illustrate the jacket of *A Suffolk Coast Garland*, published in 1928.

It was not long before the young solicitor was becoming more intimately concerned in lifeboat work. He joined the Southwold Lifeboat Committee in 1897, and three years later became secretary, a post which he held for some twenty years.

About the turn of the century Cooper took over from Walter Charles Tuck not only as Town Clerk but also as secretary to the Southwold Water Works Company, clerk to the urban sanitary authority and clerk to the school attendance committee; he added to these duties the secretaryship of the River Blyth Ferry Company and also became sub-commissioner of pilotage and before long the agent of the Shipwrecked Mariners' Society.

His maritime interests were well represented among his many posts, but it was his lifeboat work which stirred the most enthusiasm. He frequently went afloat in the lifeboat when the crew went out on exercise, and sometimes when they were called out on service. His camera would be tucked down the leg of his oilskins, often to be used in the heaviest of weather.

Lantern slides made from his pictures were given to the RNLI to be used for publicity purposes. On one occasion he was presiding at a lifeboat lecture when one of his pictures appeared on the screen; "the lecturer had no idea that the picture had been taken by his chairman," E.R. Cooper commented wryly.

His ingenuity was often tested when afloat in the lifeboat. In 1907 he went off in the boat in a gale when it was launched off the beach to take a doctor to a Swedish vessel, the *Cedric*; it was necessary to land the casualty, an injured Finnish sailor. The matter was arranged by Cooper speaking English to the captain, who interpreted in Swedish to the mate, who in turn spoke to the injured man in Russian.

During the First World War he added many other jobs to his already lengthy list, becoming commanding officer of the 3rd Volunteer Battalion, The Suffolk Regiment as well as clerk to the Military Tribunal which examined men's claims to continue working at their jobs rather than join the Forces. He also became secretary of the Canadian Relief Fund, captain of the Fire Brigade and much else.

Under wartime conditions lifeboat work became more difficult and more hazardous; years later he recalled the occasion when the boat was called out to the Glasgow steamer *Mangara*, torpedoed without warning by a U-boat a quarter-mile to seaward of the Sizewell buoy with the loss of eleven men on 28th July, 1915. By the time the lifeboat reached the scene only the masts were showing above water.

Another time he accompanied the crew to a sinking seaplane. He was on duty with the 3rd Suffolks when the call-out came, and went straight from the orderly room in his army uniform, arriving just in time to make a pierhead jump into the boat as she sailed down the harbour. The younger men were away on war service and more than once it proved extremely difficult to raise a crew, which created a serious problem for the secretary.

The last time he went out on service was in 1932, when he was in his sixties. He was in the *Mary Scott*, the first motor lifeboat stationed at Southwold, when she towed a yacht into harbour after finding her anchored in a dangerous spot.

In the midst of so busy a life he found time to write for local newspapers, yachting magazines and other periodicals. His series of articles in the *East Anglian Daily Times* under the name "Suffolk Coast" are still remembered by older members of the community.

His books display the breadth of his interests. *A Suffolk Coast Garland,* for instance, contains chapters on the Dutch wars, ghosts, smuggling stories, the Suffolk Militia and the Loyal Suffolk Hussars, old-time navigation and East Anglian trading tokens. Yet he claimed that book to be no more than "a kite flown by its author in the hope that it may influence someone, learned in research work, and with more ability and opportunity, to delve into the records relating to the once important seaports of a county which in early days, in industry, navigation, and prosperity, was second only to Middlesex-cum-London".

By his death in 1948, said the writer of an obituary in the *East Anglian Daily Times*, "Suffolk loses a rich and genial personality, imbued with a devotion to his native county and endowed with a rich store of knowledge concerning county history and especially the coast". How true that was.

Another of E.R. Cooper's remarkable photographs, taken from on board the *Alfred Corry* on service. In this instance it is to the brig *Primrose* of Folkstone in Solebay.

1 Joshua Chard, the Suffolk Hero

THE BEACHMEN and lifeboatmen of the Suffolk coast, of whom
very little has ever been written, all belonged to a class which has been
somewhat unkindly referred to as "Longshore Sharks", and whose
ancestors were labelled "a surly, savage race" by old Crabbe in his crabby
way. Nevertheless, these men in their humble, rough fashion performed
countless acts of heroism, made possible by such skill, hardihood and
invincible courage in the face of the mighty ocean as few other callings
have equalled. A few notes of some were contributed to the *Suffolk Times
and Mercury* by the late Sam Smythe in the eighteen-nineties.

I would like to recall some of the tough old beachmen of those bygone
days when our coastal waters were thronged with small, short-handed, ill-
found sailing craft, and when every breeze took its toll among the coasting
fleet, both of ships and lives.

By a strange chance the most distinguished of our nineteenth-century
longshoremen was a Dorset man who, reared on this bleak east coast,
grew up to be a true storm warrior, fearless, indomitable and ever ready,
one who earned by popular acclaim the honourable title of "The Suffolk
Hero". The title and his legendary fame have always interested me. So far as
I know no other man has borne that honour, although in 1839 a schooner
was built at Woodbridge and christened *The Suffolk Hero*, perhaps after
some earlier but now-forgotten holder of the title.

Joshua Chard was born at Netherbury, Dorset, in 1812, the youngest
of eleven, and when aged three he was brought to Stone Cottage,
Aldringham, by his mother's sister, Mrs. Osborne, who lived there and had
recently lost her own small son. So he grew up within sound of that sea
from which so many Dorset folk also wrested their living, including Sir
Samuel Hood, Nelson's admiral, and his brother sailors, who were all born

at that same village of Netherbury.

Although bound to a carpenter at Leiston, Joshua found the salt water in his blood and the call of the nearby sea too imperative to be resisted; so, soon after his time was out, Chard bought a boat for fifty shillings and started the trade of bumboatman, supplying necessaries and waiting upon the shipping in Aldeburgh and Sizewell bays, varied by an occasional sly bit of smuggling.

Chard's intimate acquaintance with every nook on the Suffolk shore and every bank at sea made him a valuable assistant in the landing of smuggled goods, and his services were often in request by the shore gangs. On one occasion he was employed to meet a Dutch vessel off Lowestoft, probably one of the copers which worked among the smacks on the Dogger, so Chard launched his big boat, fitted out with lines, anchors and fishing gear complete, and sailed away on the ebb tide so as to get well to the Norrard.

They fetched Lowestoft in due course and put in there to buy some skate and other fish so as to have a catch to land on their return. Chard then stood off into the sea and, finding the Dutchman at the agreed rendezvous, took on board 25cwt of tobacco in bales; he then squared away for home, and a nice easterly breeze coming in carried him to Sizewell before dark, and too soon for a landing.

He therefore proposed they should land and shove the boat off again, to ride at anchor till the time arranged. Unfortunately she took the beach with too much way and, after they had jumped ashore, could not be got afloat again. Then the sea getting up a bit, it broke over the stern and the boat began to fill.

As bad luck would have it, the Preventive men from Thorpe and Sizewell had just made a meeting on the Cliff, and on his way home the Thorpe man came down off the cliff and steered straight for the boat. Chard found himself between the devil and the deep blue sea in very truth, but, risking all on a bold stroke, he ran to meet the officer. In a state of great agitation, he begged him as a friend to hurry to Thorpe and ask some of the fishermen to come quickly with his big crab chain so that they could haul the boat out of the breakers and save his little all from destruction.

The man fell into Chard's artful trap and set off running his hardest; as soon as he was round the Ness Chard and his crew set to work, got out the wet bales and carried them up the beach. Then the sails, lines, fish and all the gear were landed and dumped on top of the tobacco, after which Chard produced a can of tar from the cuddy and upset it in the boat to change the colour of the tobacco-stained water.

By that time the Thorpemen had arrived; having got the boat up and let the water out, they launched her again to ride afloat. Then Chard invited everybody to Mrs. Watson's beerhouse to have a gallon at his expense. So off they set, but it coming dark Chard made an excuse to return to the boat. Within an hour the "spotsman", who had been watching the proceedings from his hideyhole on the cliff, had collected his gang and the whole of the tobacco was safely run, thanks to the ready wit and innocent-seeming craftiness of the simple fisherman.

It was not long before he was able to buy a faster and better boat, an ex-smuggler called the *Venus*, and in addition he invested in a coasting pilot book and chart of the Thames Estuary and set up as an unlicensed pilot for the London River. These men who held no warrants from Trinity House were generally called "Brums", otherwise "Brummagem pilots".

Chard's next boat was aptly named *Stormy Petrel*, and right well she and her gallant owner lived up to the name. Many ships he piloted to safety in the absence of Trinity pilots, and sometimes in their presence, for which he was hauled up before Newson Garrett, then ruler of pilots at Aldeburgh; but he generally got off with a caution. One of his star jobs was in 1864, when he took charge of the 74-gun HMS *Edinburgh* and piloted her to a safe anchorage. Twenty years earlier, when Sir John Franklin had set out on his last and fatal voyage, the *Erebus* and *Terror* anchored in the bay on 20th May, 1845, and lay there a week windbound. Chard was first alongside and was employed to supply fish and fresh provisions during their stay. He was therefore one of the very last to see the explorers before they sailed, never to return.

Chard once went off in a very rough sea to a vessel making signals, apparently for a pilot. Going alongside, he was rudely received by the captain, who presented a pistol at his head and threatened to blow out his brains if he did not clear out instantly. Chard pushed off without delay, but he took a careful description of the ship and proceeded straightaway to Lowestoft, whence he was hurried off to the London Custom House. The information he gave led to the vessel being arrested on arrival, and proving to be a smuggler the blustering captain was fined £50.

On Valentine's Day, 1860, while piloting the barque *James White* to

London, he sighted and rescued a boatful of sailormen who had lost their ship on the Sunk Sand the night before.

In 1849 Chard began to keep a journal, from which a brief account of his later life was published after his death. Through the kindness of "Rambler" of the *East Anglian Daily Times* I am able to quote some of the outstanding jobs there recorded. For instance, on 7th November, 1849, Joshua and his crew of Thorpe men saved eight men from the brig *Olive Branch* on Sizewell Bank, and on 7th December, 1851, they rescued the captain and crew of the brig *John*, sunk on Thorpe Rocks. For this rescue our hero was awarded the silver medal of the Royal National Lifeboat Institution, and his name stands for all time on their roll of honour. He also received the Royal Humane Society's medal for one of his many rescues.

On a Sunday morning, 19th December, 1852, the brig *Ann & Mary*, of Sunderland, bound from her home port to London, struck on Sizewell Bank and sank. The crew, with the exception of the mate, took to the boats, but a schooner which went to the aid of the small boat collided with it, causing it to overturn; only two of the occupants were picked up. Joshua Chard saw what had happened and launched his boat with a crew of four, took the mate off the topgallant yard of the brig and then searched for and picked up the captain, who, more dead than alive, was clinging to an oar. They were then abreast of Southwold, and fearing the captain would die before he could make Lowestoft Chard made for the beach there; although waved off from the cliff, he succeeded in making a safe landing through a raging sea and, thanks to prompt attention, both the men recovered. Three other men in the long boat were picked up by the Southwold yawl *Friendship*, belonging to the Kilcock Cliff Company.

Chard and his crew next saved eight men from the brig *Montcalm*, of Shields, in January, 1853. When the first of three lifeboats named *Ipswich*, known as the Blue lifeboat, was placed at Thorpe that year Chard was coxswain of her for a time, but most of his work was done in his own boats.

When one day in 1855 a Thorpe fisherman, John Barker, fell overboard and could not get aboard again Chard observed him from the shore. He went off at once and arrived just in time to save him. On 28th May of that same year Chard boarded the ss *Lion*, ashore on the Ness, his boat being capsized and the crew in great danger while alongside. They got the steamer off and anchored her in safety, being awarded salvage on a value of £24,000. Chard promptly spent his share on another boat.

At daybreak on 3rd May, 1860, he saw a brig, the *Vanguard*, of Whitby, on Thorpe Rocks and at once floated his boat and rescued the crew of seven just before the brig sank. As his boat would not hold all hands, he sent her to lie inside the Shoal while he took the *Vanguard's* boat across, and all got ashore in safety. Two years later he assisted the Thorpe lifeboat in the rescue of the crew of the *Henry Morton*, but shortly afterwards when assisting the *Hope*, of Glasgow, which was fast on the shoal, Chard's boat was capsized. A man named Parker lost his life while carrying out anchors and chain across the shoal, the only fatality which attended Chard's many services; he had orders to cross the same way they came, but elected to go a shorter road.

In 1862 the brig *Dora*, of Exeter, struck on Sizewell Bank during a gale. Chard promptly launched and boarded her, and by trimming the sails he forced the ship off the bank. Then, however, she made so much water that he was obliged to run her aground on Sizewell beach, getting all hands ashore in safety. The next year he boarded the Hamburg ship *Andrew*, ashore at Thorpe Haven, after the rocket line had been sent over her, and instructed and helped the crew to work the line, by which means the whole crew of eighteen was saved.

There were many other occasions when Joshua, in his own boat, in the lifeboat, or with the rocket brigade, helped to save life. Such was his fame that after the loss of his latest boat in 1869 a public subscription was raised throughout the county, the list being headed by the Bishop of Norwich, the Mayor of Ipswich, the Members of Parliament, the Reverend Richard Cobbold, and many other prominent Ipswich and Suffolk people, 150 all told, who put up some £200 to be spent on the building of a 28-foot lifeboat by Hunt, of Aldeburgh, suitable both for fishing and lifesaving. This boat was presented to Chard by Mrs. Margaret Ogilvie of Sizewell Hall on 19th May, 1870, and was duly christened *Rescue* before being launched from Sizewell beach in the presence of about five thousand people who had assembled to do honour to the county hero of the coast.

It was then stated that the Suffolk Hero had been instrumental in saving, or assisting to save, 109 lives, eighty of these men having been rescued by him in his own boats. He had also taken charge of more than a hundred vessels requiring pilots and had brought them to their port or to a safe anchorage. It is probable that few if any longshoremen in Great Britain have left such a record of service to seamankind.

While this testimonial was maturing the Reverend Richard Cobbold, the author of *Margaret Catchpole* and other popular Victorian novels, who was quite at home on that corner of our coast, interested himself in doing three watercolour drawings of Joshua himself and of two outstanding episodes in his adventurous career. More than half a century later these drawings were still treasured in the family.

It was a tragedy that when this fine old seadog was in peril himself there was not a soul about to lend him a rescuing hand. So, alone in the darkness of a wild December night, he met the fate from which he had snatched so many in his time. The *Ipswich Journal* prefaced its report of the tragedy with the words:

> We chronicle to-day with the greatest regret the violent and untimely death of one of the most courageous sons of the sea who ever risked his life in battling with the waves to rescue perishing fellow creatures.

It seems that on 20th December, 1875, Chard piloted a steamboat to Gravesend and telegraphed home that he had arrived safely. It is supposed that he sailed again at once, for an Aldeburgh pilot, bound up, saw him in his boat near the Spitway. Late that night the boat was found full of water between Aldeburgh and Thorpe; it had no doubt been swamped when crossing the shoal.

Early next morning Chard's body was found at Thorpe, not far from his home. There were signs on the beach that he had reached the shore and had tried to crawl to safety, but for want of a helping hand he was swept away again, and so perished.

Joshua and his wife lie together in the lonely, peaceful God's acre at Aldringham, under a simple cross inscribed:

> In loving memory of Joshua Chard, the Suffolk Hero, who was found drowned on Thorpe beach December 21st, 1875, aged 63 years.

The stone was put up by James Smythe, of Aldeburgh, and made by Allen, of Southwold, two towns where he is still remembered with pride.

Chard's widow lived on until 1896, and is alluded to on the cross as "An

Opposite: Plans of a Beeching self-righting lifeboat similar to the *Harriett*, acquired by the Southwold Lifeboat Society in 1852.

Plate I.

LIFE BOAT, BY JAMES BEECHING, G? YARMOUTH.

Submitted to compete for the Northumberland Premium.

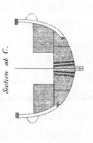

Section at 3.

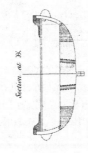

Section at 8.

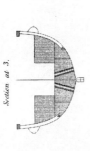

Section at C.

Shear Plan.

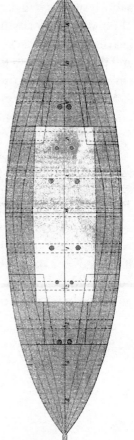

Plan.

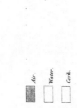

Body Plan.

Aft Fore

Air.
Water.
Cork.

PRINCIPAL DIMENSIONS

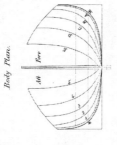

Length extreme .... 36 ft. 6 ins.
Length of Keel .... 34 . 0 .
Breadth of Beam .... 9 . 6 .
Depth .... 3 . 6 .
Sheer of Gunwale .... 3 . 0 .
Extra Buoyancy .No:M? Cubic ft. .... 8¼ tons
Internal capacity up to the level of the thwarts 5
Area of delivering tubes .... 256 Sq. ins
Proportion of delivering area to capacity .... 4 to 6½
Weight of Boat or displacement .... 3¼ tons
Ballast 2 tons of Water & iron keel 1 ton 2½
Draught of Water with 32 men on board .... 2 ft. 2 ins.
N? of Overdouble haschel 12
Clinch built of Oak & iron fastened ....
Rig of Boat .... 2 lug sails
Cost complete .... £ 250

Scale ¼ Inch to a Foot

Jas: by Joseph Prowse of H.M. Dockyard, Woolwich, 1851

Standidge & C? Litho: Old Jewry

old disciple". Postcards in memory of the Suffolk Hero were published and sold for the benefit of the widow; I expect some are still treasured by old-timers.

The boat from which Chard was lost was not the presentation *Rescue* but a much smaller one named *Surprise*, which could be worked single handed. Those who know anything of longshoring will understand that a 28-foot heavily-built lifeboat could only be launched and handled with ample help, and that according to the custom of the coast anyone involved in the operation who laid a finger on the boat when going off would claim a dole from the earnings. Thus it was greatly to Chard's interest to use his small boat whenever possible. After her owner was lost the *Rescue* was sold and went, I am told, to France as a yacht.

The astonishing thing is that in the midst of this intensely active life of peril, adventure and anxiety, Chard and his wife brought up a family of fourteen; in those days children were considered a good investment.

The last survivor of that family was Mrs. Lavinia King, who when I met her at the age of eighty-six was spending the evening of a long and useful life in peace and content in that same little village by the North Sea. When I inquired if she had seen the wartime wreck of the *Carmenta* near by, at which the Southwold lifeboat was nearly lost, she made answer quite simply: "No, I never go on the beach since poor father was lost."

2 Ben Herrington and John Cragie

FOR OVER three hundred years the name of Herrington is found in the annals of Southwold. The registers show that Robert Herrington was baptized there in 1607; Stephen Herrington was a bailiff in 1609; and that same year a Stephen, probably the bailiff's son, was married. From their connection with the Bemond, or Beamont, and Jentilman families I suspect they were of Dunwich ancestry, and men of the sea from "time whereof the memory of man runneth not to the contrary."

The first Ben Herrington seems to have been born in 1680, since when there has been a succession of Bens. I have known three of them—"Old Bennicks", "Young Bennicks" and the "Boy Benny"—all now gone aloft to join Tom Bowling, perhaps a little lost in the realm where "there shall be no more sea."

The subject of this memoir is Benjamin, son of Benjamin, born in a house on the beach at Southwold in the early teens of the nineteenth century, and who took to the sea like a "willock." I remember him late in life, stalwart, bull-chested, with a mane like a lion, and ready even then to take a bear by the beard at a moment's notice. As a boy he was up to a little bit of "daviltry" now and again, and his name appears in Southwold Gaol Book in 1825 when, with three other young rips, he was gaoled "for two hours only, for daubing the gate and posts"; a salutary warning.

After various coasting voyages Ben was in 1835 a bluejacket in HMS *Pique* (Captain the Hon. H.J. Rous, of Henham), then bound for Lisbon and the Spanish coast. Ben was one of his captain's boat's crew, and I have an extract from a letter from Captain Rous describing him as a fine fellow, and adding that he had two more Southwold lads who would turn out well.

Captain Rous was a son of the first Earl of Stradbroke, and became Admiral Rous, so well known on Newmarket Heath; the *Pique* was the famous 36-gun frigate launched at Plymouth in 1834, known in the service as the "Spit and Polish *Pique*" and celebrated in a song of twelve verses:

> Oh, 'tis of a fine frigate, La Pique was her name,
> All in the West Indies she bore a great name,
> For cruel bad usage of every degree,
> Like slaves in the galley we ploughed the salt sea.

There was a painting of her at Henham, showing that excessive smartness which proved too much for our Ben, who deserted when she returned to Spithead and got safely out of Portsmouth disguised as a tinker. He then tramped to London Docks and shipped in a purser's name aboard a barque bound to America. Their next voyage was to Quebec, where by chance they anchored just below the *Pique*, and Ben had a very narrow squeak from being caught. However, he escaped and so missed helping to get the frigate off the Labrador rocks and to bring her home without a rudder and with a rock sticking through her bottom; the rock is still preserved in Portsmouth Dockyard in honour of that feat of seamanship.

About the time of Queen Victoria's Coronation, which took place in 1837, the senior Benjamin Herrington died and his son returned to Southwold to carry on the family business of longshoring; very soon he was made second coxswain of the lifeboat. He evidently imported some of the *Pique's* smartness, as in 1845 the Southwold lifeboat *Solebay* competed against the boats from Pakefield, Lowestoft and Yarmouth at Yarmouth Regatta and won the third prize of £4 10s. The lifeboats at Lowestoft and Pakefield were then maintained by the Suffolk Humane Society and the Yarmouth boats and others in Norfolk by the Norfolk Shipwreck Association, while little Southwold had to provide and maintain its own boat under constant financial difficulties. In 1846, too, the Southwold boat was awarded first prize for superiority in the management of the boat at Lowestoft Regatta.

While second coxswain of the *Solebay* Herrington took part in several thrilling rescues, particularly that of the rescue of the crew of nine from the brig *Cleofrid.* in 1848. Following that rescue the captain of the brig wrote the following to the *Shipping Gazette*:

> I, the undersigned, James Simm, Master of the Brig Cleofrid, of
> Newcastle, wrecked on Sizewell Bank, on Tuesday, the 21st day of March

inst., do hereby testify that it is my firm belief that myself and crew, consisting of nine hands, including myself, were saved on that day by the means of the Southwold Lifeboat and the gallant exertions of her crew, and I do also hereby tender my thanks on behalf of myself and my said crew for the kind assistance and relief that we received from Mr Read Crisp, Lloyd's Agent, and F. W. Willis, Esq., Receiver of Droits of Admiralty, the Mayor of the said Borough, the gentry and other inhabitants of Southwold generally.

As witness my hand the day and year above written.

JAMES SIMM

On 21st August, 1848, a barque was riding out a south-westerly gale in the Bay and it was observed she had a flag in the foretopgallant rigging. The lifeboat was launched and the vessel was found to be the *Mary Bulwer*, of Newcastle, and in want of a pilot; after a pilot had been put on board the lifeboat returned ashore. In those days the crew who went off to a wreck received £5 among them, and the floaters received nothing; apparently on this occasion even the £5 was missing as the coxswains applied to the committee to know how they were to be paid, and they were referred to a lawyer.

Another rescue in which Benjamin Herrington took part was that from the schooner *Ury* of Sunderland, bound to Dunkirk with coal, which struck on the Barnard at four in the morning on 4th December, 1848. At 8am she was observed from Kessingland dismasted, but the Kessingland men found there was too much sea for them to launch their yawl and a man was sent on horseback to Southwold.

The Southwold lifeboat was launched successfully and took about half an hour to reach the wreck, which was on her broadside with the decks blown out and a tremendous sea breaking over her. The coxswain anchored her to windward and veered her down towards the wreck, first rescuing a man who was fast to a rope among the wreckage. Ropes were thrown to another man, but he was insensible; John Fish, one of the lifeboatmen, got on to one of the masts that was floating, still attached to the wreck by the rigging, and by running along it succeeded in reaching the unconscious man. It was no easy matter even to break his grip of the rigging, and getting him back to the lifeboat was a dangerous and difficult job indeed.

Commander Richard Joachim, who was in command of the Coastguard at Lowestoft and himself sometimes took charge of the Lowestoft lifeboat *Victoria*, gave the coxswain this certificate of service:

The Southwold Lifeboat landed here this morning two seamen in a very exhausted state whom the crew of the Lifeboat had rescued from a vessel sunk on the Barnard, and having questioned the rescued men on the subject, I have every reason to believe the crew of the Lifeboat performed their work in a very meritorious manner.

R. JOACHIM, R.N.

A less scholarly but infinitely more moving letter was received by Benjamin Herrington from the rescued men after their return home:

SUNDERLAND
       December 14th, 1848

Dear Friends,
I have taken this favourable opportunity of writing to you these few lines hoping this will find you all in good health as leaves booth of us great deal better than we was, when we got home we was very stif with the bruses we had about us we arrived safe home the thursday night we have had a letter saying that the master is picked up his brother went away directly to see him buried if ever you go to lowstoft give our kind love to the landlord for his kindness to us I hope god will reward you for all your kindness toward us Give my kind love to that man that took me of the wreck, but not to him alone but to you all So no more at present but ever remain your wellwishers.
CHARLES HOLLEY and JOHN COURTNELL

For this particularly gallant deed Lloyd's Committee voted £19 10s. (£19.50) to the lifeboat crew, £5 of which was for John Fish, who was also awarded the National Shipwreck Institution's silver medal.

On 24th November, 1851, the *Latona* of Hull, on a voyage to that port from Quebec with timber, struck on the south end of the Barnard about 5am during a strong wind at SSE and was abandoned by her crew. At daylight she was discovered from Southwold and the lifeboat went off to her. Finding nobody on board, the lifeboatmen took possession and succeeded in floating the vessel on the flowing tide, bringing her to anchor off Southwold; as she was completely waterlogged and difficult to steer they hired steam tugs to tow her to Lowestoft the following day.

The amount of salvage awarded was £650, and the Solemen doled £6 a share; three shares, £18, went to the lifeboat society, which by its rules was

The Southwold lifeboat *Harriett* launched to the aid of a ship aground on the Outer Shoal in 1852, an engraving from the *Illustrated London News*.

entitled to three shares for the use of the lifeboat in such circumstances. Had the beachmen used one of their yawls for a similar service the beach company would have been entitled to a similar payment for the upkeep of the boat.

The *William Cook*, of Yarmouth, bound from Hartlepool with coal for Ramsgate, struck on the outer shoal abreast of the town on 11th January, 1852, the wind blowing a gale from the south with a heavy sea and thick with rain. The lifeboat made four attempts to reach the vessel, at first under oars and then with sails. At the third attempt the crew succeeded in saving the master, but the fourth time the boat filled, the air tanks gave way and the crew were obliged to run her ashore. The remainder of the crew, with the exception of one man who was drowned when he fell from the bowsprit, were brought ashore by Manby's lifesaving mortar apparatus.

Ben Herrington was promoted coxswain in 1852, and along with a new coxswain the Southwold Lifeboat Society acquired a new lifeboat, for the *Solebay* was found to be in need of extensive repairs after the service to the *William Cook*. Thinking it better to build a new boat on improved principles than to repair the old one, the society opened a subscription list headed by Miss Harriett Sheriffe, who lived at Centre Cliff, Southwold, and Sir Edward Gooch, of Benacre Hall, with £100 each, and immediately ordered a self-righting boat to be built by James Beeching, of Yarmouth.

Beeching had the year before received the Duke of Northumberland's prize of a hundred guineas (£105) for a new and more effective type of lifeboat; his was in fact the first effective self-righting boat. The Southwold Lifeboat Society paid £280 for the new craft, which was constructed of oak to his prize-winning design and was the largest boat of her type. The new boat was christened *Harriett* after Lady Gooch and Miss Sheriffe on 8th October, 1852. With the introduction of the new boat the society drew up new rules for the working of the lifeboat, and Herrington's name appears as coxswain in the list of crew members appended to the new rules.

The *Harriett* was first launched on service on 29th November, 1853, when about 4pm a brig was seen drifting towards the town in a strong SSW gale with a flag of distress in her rigging. The fishermen prepared to launch the yawl *John Bull*, but the report in a local newspaper says they "were deterred from doing so by a large body of females who, apprehensive of the danger, created a panic." The lifeboat was thereupon launched, it being then dark, and after an hour's struggle against sea and wind the lifeboatmen reached the vessel to find her deserted, with the sea washing over her. It was discovered that the crew had taken to the longboat, so the lifeboatmen dropped astern and rescued the whole nine men.

The lifeboatmen tried to save the vessel, the *Sheraton Grange*, from Sunderland for London with coal, but presently she struck and became a total wreck. For this rescue Herrington and the second coxswain, William Waters, both received medals from the RNLI, which were presented to them at a dinner at the Old Swan given by Miss Sheriffe to celebrate the event.

The newspaper report concludes with the hope that "the present happy result will give the crew that confidence in their noble boat which she so well merits." Unfortunately the hopes expressed by the newspaper and all interested in the lifeboat society were not realised, for the crew expressed dissatisfaction at the sailing and seakeeping properties of the new boat, and eventually refused to go off in the *Harriett*, whatever alterations might be made in her. At the same time, strangely enough, they declared themselves quite willing and ready to go off in the old boat, notwithstanding that she had been practically condemned.

It seems likely that the men's dissatisfaction stemmed not only from problems with their own new self-righting boat but also from the news that smaller boats of a similar design built by Beeching for the Shipwrecked Fishermen's and Mariners' Benevolent Society and stationed at Lytham in Lancashire and Rhyl in Wales had overturned.

The Southwold Lifeboat Society found itself in a dilemma; it possessed two lifeboats, one considered unseaworthy which the men were quite willing to use, and the other a brand-new self-righting boat of the latest type which the men absolutely refused to go off in. As might be expected, not only had the society no funds to make use of but they still owed Beeching £30 on account of the *Harriett*. They took the wisest course possible under these circumstances and applied to the RNLI for advice and assistance.

Ultimately the Institution offered to contribute £200 towards the building of a new boat which should be satisfactory to the men and to take over the Southwold society with its assets and liabilities provided the committee would have the boat built and find the rest of the money required. This offer was considered at a general meeting of the Southwold Lifeboat Society on 21st October, 1854, and was unanimously accepted.

After fourteen years of very useful work, harassed throughout by lack of funds, this gallant little society, one of the pioneers of lifesaving work, made its bow and the Southwold station became the Southwold branch of the Royal National Lifeboat Institution. It was endowed with fresh energy and better finances.

The first lifeboat built for Southwold through the RNLI, a non-self-righting boat of the Norfolk and Suffolk type built of oak by James Beeching at Yarmouth, was delivered on the last day of 1855. Like her predecessor she took the name of *Harriett*, and did good service at Southwold until 1893.

The *Solebay* was sold for £45 to Kessingland, where she continued to serve until 1869, but no purchaser could be found for the self-righting *Harriett*. After many fruitless attempts to sell her the Southwold Lifeboat Association gave her to the RNLI and she left the harbour for London on 15th February, 1857. The Institution altered her and sent her to Yarmouth the following year; in 1860 she was transferred to Wexford in Ireland.

A dispute arose between the lifeboat committee and the crew regarding a salvage award made in the case of the brig *Pensher*, of and from Sunderland for London, coal laden, which was found with seven feet of water in her on the night of 9th February, 1857. It was blowing hard at SSW when the lifeboat arrived; although the captain said that she was sinking fast, twenty men jumped from the lifeboat on board her and worked at the pumps until she was got safely into Lowestoft and put on the ground. The salvage awarded was £200 and the lifeboat's share £38 12s. 6d., the best haul the funds ever received until the Institution abandoned any share in salvage money.

The rights and wrongs of the case are long forgotten, but Ben Herrington attended a meeting with a sense of injustice and the key of the boathouse in his pocket. His contribution to the discussion was to thump the key on the table and inform the startled gentry, in the bluntest of sailor lingo, exactly what they could do with it. There was also a fuss with a Coastguard officer who interfered at a launch, upon which Ben loudly declared that he was AB aboard Her Majesty's ships before the other's stern was wet with salt water.

The result of this clash was that for three years Ben was out of office, but he carried on his work in the beach yawls *Reliance* and *Jubilee* and the gigs belonging to the Long Island Cliff Company, with which many daring and profitable jobs were performed in those rough old days alongshore. On one occasion he was in charge of the *Jubilee* when she was capsized by a heavy sea while launching. All got clear except Edward Palmer, who was under the boat; when the planking of the boat was cut through with axes he was found to be dead, with one of the finest agates ever seen on that beach in his mouth.

The Norfolk and Suffolk type lifeboats were fine craft, of that there is no doubt, but the loose water ballast swilling about in the bottom of the boat could in some circumstances prove a source of danger. This was tragically illustrated on Saturday, 27th February, 1858, when a most lamentable accident resulted in the drowning of three gentlemen as the lifeboat was returning from exercise.

An eyewitness has told me it was a beautiful day with a fresh breeze at ENE and rather a rough sea which caused the waves to break on the shoal, but not by any means bad for a lifeboat. It appears from the evidence that the crew had put in the plugs and baled and pumped most of the water out of her, leaving about 8in of water in. The coxswain, Francis Cooper (this was during Ben Herrington's three years in the wilderness), stated that he felt the rudder, which hung 2ft below the keel, touch the ground, but there appears to be no doubt that the boat ran on a breaking sea on the shoal which lifted her stern and shot what water there was all into her bows.

The weight being then all for'd, she broached to, broadside on to the sea. The following sea broke over her and into the sails, and she went over on her side. She remained in that position about five minutes, but as soon as her masts touched the ground they broke off and she capsized completely, drifting ashore bottom up. The men were all thrown into the sea except one visitor, the Reverend Robert Hodges, the young curate of Wangford, who was found dead under the boat with his legs entangled in the gear.

The lifeboatmen, all of them wearing the heavy and cumbersome cork lifebelts, were all saved, five by swimming to the shore and the others by their fellow-beachmen of the Long Island Cliff Company, who launched the yawl *Reliance* to their assistance. The gentlemen, George Ellis, the eighteen-year-old son of Captain Francis Ellis, who was surveyor of Southwold harbour and Lloyd's Agent, and seventeen-year-old John Henry Ord, did not have lifebelts on and were both drowned. Benjamin Herrington was one of those who gave evidence at the inquest.

Full inquiries were made by Admiral Thomas Hardy and Captain Ward of the RNLI, who entirely exonerated the local officials from any blame and gave it as their opinion that the accident was caused by the boat running too fast before a broken sea in shoal water, aided by the loose water ballast rushing to the bows, which they pointed out was one of the defects of that class of boat. Captain Ward stated that he remembered a large yawl being lost at Aldeburgh some years earlier in exactly the same way, and he thought the coxswain should have reduced sail before getting into broken water.

As a result of the accident various alterations were made in the *Harriett*, the chief modification being the making of bulkheads across the well with solid chocks of wood weighted to the specific gravity of water. The men seem to have had their confidence in the boat quite restored by these changes, which were put to a severe test in the harbour on 19th May, when the boat refused to capsize even with thirty-two men standing on one gunwale and thirty-six others hauling on a rope from the masthead.

Herrington was in the crew when the lifeboat received a much severer test on 17th September, 1859, after being launched to a vessel ashore at Misner Haven in a heavy gale at N by W. The boat was launched at 10.30pm and the lifeboatmen found the wreck, which proved to be the Prussian brig *Lucinde*, belonging to Memel, about midnight. She had been bound to Rochester with a cargo of railway sleepers.

One man had already been drowned before the lifeboat arrived, and the whole crew must have had a terrible experience for some eight or nine

John Cragie, who took over from Ben Herrington as coxswain of the Southwold lifeboat in 1879, having been second coxswain for 20 years before that.

hours. A rocket line had been thrown to the wreck by the lifesaving apparatus team on the beach, but it seems that the men on the *Lucinde* had no idea what to do with it; Joshua Chard, who was with the LSA team, advised that they should break the line and wait for the lifeboat, but it was a long time coming. A messenger would take not less than two hours to get from Misner to Southwold, then an hour would be occupied in launching, and the lifeboat would have taken three hours getting there and rescuing the crew, and all this time the sea was making a complete breach over the masthead of the wrecked ship.

With much difficulty the lifeboatmen saved the remaining ten men of the crew and the captain's wife, who was quite exhausted. As the boat was being beached on Misner beach at about one in the morning a huge sea swept John Cragie, who was acting coxswain that night, overboard; he hung tight to the tiller and managed to haul himself back into the boat.

John Cragie was awarded the RNLI's silver medal and Benjamin Herrington received the second service clasp to the silver medal he had won in 1853. The Institution also awarded the crew double pay, £30, and the lifeboatmen received Bibles "most splendidly bound." In addition the Prussian Consul sent £30 for the crew, and a visitor collected a purse of £20 for them in London, so this gallant deed did not go unrewarded. On the other hand, some of the men who left on a private expedition by land to the wreck as soon as the news arrived in Southwold were forthwith struck off the strength of the crews.

Peace was made in 1860, and Ben was reappointed coxswain, so he was in charge on the morning of 28th January, 1862, when after a blowing night the men on lookout in the cliff-houses observed a boat drifting outside the inner shoal. The lifeboat was launched at 7.30am and rescued the crew of five men and a dog from the boat of the Ipswich schooner *Princess Alice*, which had struck on Sizewell Bank about 1.30am and had immediately filled and sunk; the crew had taken to the boat and had drifted all night in the greatest danger.

There is no record of any further service until 24th January, 1865, when the boat assisted to save the brig *Elizabeth*, of Lowestoft, which was on her way from Newcastle with coal for Southampton. The Southwold men took her to Harwich. On this occasion the crew got into disgrace for settling the salvage claim without consulting the committee; the share received by the branch was £14 7s.

Sometimes the heroism of the lifeboatmen and the exertions of their helpers ashore went unrewarded, as they did on 13th January, 1866, when about 11am a brig was observed running before a south-westerly gale with an ensign in her rigging. The lifeboat crew was immediately summoned, but before they could get the boat off the brig struck on the inner shoal opposite the town, and her masts immediately went overboard. The lifeboat crossed the shoal and her anchor was let go to windward, but owing to the violence of the wind and sea the anchor would not hold and she missed the wreck. The coxswain took her back across the shoal and fifty men on the beach towed the boat up again into a position from which she could reach the wreck. The sails were set, close reefed, and the boat sailed off again outside the wreck.

Once more the lifeboatmen let go the anchor, veering away 60 or 70 fathoms of cable. Again the anchor would not hold, and the lifeboat drove past the wreck a second time. The men on shore set to work again to tow the lifeboat up to windward. Before the boat sailed off for a third time another anchor was put on board, and this time both anchors were let go. The sea broke clean over the lifeboat as she was veered down to the wreck, but by this time all the crew except one had been washed overboard and drowned.

The lifeboatmen hailed the survivor, telling him to go to the stern so that they could rescue him from there. He was in the act of climbing on to the stern when a sea carried him overboard, and although the cable was cut immediately so that the lifeboat could go to his aid he sank before it reached him. The lifeboat was beached in front of the town at 3pm.

The lifeboatmen had spent four hours in the boat and had made the most strenuous efforts to save the distressed crew in a sea which the veteran Ben Herrington declared was the heaviest he had ever been off in. Some time later a small boat was washed ashore from the wreck, and from this it was ascertained that the brig was the *Billy*, of Whitby, which had attained the respectable age of fifty-five before bringing disaster upon herself and her crew.

After this distressing event a deputation of pilots waited upon the lifeboat committee and represented the need of a surf boat which could be taken along the shore and launched immediately under the lee of a wreck. Their views were duly reported to the Institution, and after inquiries had been made it was decided to place a small rowing carriage boat, the *Quiver*, at Southwold and to build a new house for it.

During 1869 it was announced by the Institution that the coal merchants of London had raised £700 which was presented to the RNLI to defray the cost of a lifeboat establishment, and that they had decided to take up as the lifeboat the large boat stationed at Southwold. The *Harriett* was thereupon renamed the *London Coal Exchange*, by which name she was known during the remainder of her career.

The *London Coal Exchange*, ex-*Harriett*, was launched on 16th December, 1873, to the assistance of the Prussian schooner *David*, which had been seen to have a flag in her rigging as a distress signal. She had sprung a leak while on her voyage from Burghead on the Moray Firth with barley for London. The lifeboatmen were successful in saving the vessel and her crew of six, carrying her into Lowestoft. The lifeboat's share of the salvage award was £10.

The year 1874 appears to have been a record year for the number of lives saved by the Southwold lifeboat, the total for the year being twenty-five men. On 15th April a messenger sent from Thorpe at midnight alerted Ben Herrington to the fact that the barque *Alma*, of Tonsberg, had stranded on the Sizewell Bank and that the Thorpe self-righting lifeboat *Ipswich* had been launched but was unable to do anything. The *Coal Exchange* was launched and at daybreak saved nine men and the pilot, the Thorpe boat taking off the rest. Both boats had to go ashore at Aldeburgh.

Ben Herrington took the *Coal Exchange* out again on 21st October and saved the crew of five of the schooner *Pandora*, of Portsmouth, sunk on the Barnard. No sooner had they taken the five men on board than the lifeboatmen saw a three-masted schooner strike the sand close at hand. It was the *Glenville*, of London, with a crew of ten. Herrington and his crew immediately proceeded to her assistance, and succeeded in getting the vessel off and into Lowestoft harbour, where she sank. It took nearly a year to settle up the salvage claim for the *Glenville*, but in September, 1875, the lifeboat funds benefited to the extent of £36.

In 1879 "Old Bennicks" retired from his position as coxswain and was followed by his cousin John Cragie, who had for years been his second coxswain. Ben was presented with £10 and a pair of binoculars by the Institution in acknowledgement of his gallant services over a period of thirty-eight years.

Like the Herringtons, the Cragie family was among the oldest in Southwold. The family is first mentioned in 1637, when Walter Craggy married Christian Laborne, but they might well have been there ages before that. The name Crageir is found in the Icelandic sagas, the first member of the family to be mentioned having earned the name by letting himself down over the sea crags and slain seven men single handed.

A friend in the Shetlands says it was a very old family there which had only died out in the first half of the twentieth century, and that there is a

The Southwold No 1 lifeboat *Alfred Corry* running before the wind.

landing place there still called "Cragie's Stane". The first Cragie probably came to Southwold in one of the many Iceland ships which sailed from the town and from Dunwich in past centuries. These vessels often shipped Icelanders or Shetlanders to fill the places of men who died or went missing during the voyage.

The John Cragie who took over the position of coxswain in 1879 was born about 1827. Like his ancestors, he was a lifelong and successful fisherman, and also made a name for himself as a salvager and lifesaver. At the time of the gale of 28th May, 1860, long remembered for its ferocity and the destruction it caused among the coasting and fishing fleets, Cragie put to sea in his lugger *Fanny* to look for a "Gallooner". The *Fanny*, of 22 tons, was one of those light, clinker-built "half-and-halfers" built for the herring and mackerel fishing, and very buoyant sea-kindly craft they were. The name was derived from the custom of splitting the earnings equally between the owner, who was responsible for the upkeep of boat and fishing gear, and the crew.

Cragie and his crew first fell in with the Lowestoft lugger *Post Boy*, clean swept, and assisted her into Lowestoft harbour. Then Cragie ran off into the sea and found the Sandwich brig *Hannah*, waterlogged, with a flag in her rigging. They took off the crew of seven just before she went down.

The *Fanny* then reached to the northward and her crew boarded the *Three Brothers*, of Goole, derelict, her crew having been rescued by the Lowestoft lifeboat. They towed her into Sole Bay, landed the *Hannah's* crew, and then two days afterwards got the *Three Brothers* safely into Southwold harbour. This was really useful salvage work, which one hopes was well rewarded.

On another occasion when out in his punt John Cragie went to the brig *Cowan*, which had been run ashore leaking, and took off her crew of seven and three smacksmen who had been employed to help at the pumps. Another time when he was out fishing his punt capsized, and that time it was Cragie himself who was saved, by a Whitstable smack.

John Cragie had been a member of the lifeboat crew since he was seventeen, and had been acting coxswain on that dreadful night in 1859 when the crew of the Prussian brig *Lucinde* and the captain's wife were rescued and landed on Misner beach at one in the morning. He was appointed second coxswain in 1860.

The lifeboats effected many useful services during Cragie's time as

John Cragie after his retirement in 1898.

coxswain, one of them during a memorable easterly gale and blizzard on 18th January, 1881, said to have been the heaviest within living memory. At the height of the gale a barque was driven upon the shoal opposite Centre Cliff, Miss Harriett Sheriffe's home. Her masts soon went over the side, and the cries of the crew, who were seen hanging on as best they might, could be heard from the shore.

The *Quiver* was got out, horses were procured, and she was dragged up into the town in order to get on to the shore under the lee of the vessel, but before she could be got into position the vessel went to pieces and all the crew disappeared. Only three survivors were washed ashore, and they were in a terrible state. One of them was taken in by the Herringtons, who nursed him back to health and strength.

The *London Coal Exchange* was floated on 4th April, 1882, to the aid of three men in a Southwold punt, one of the numerous little lugsail fishing boats then working off the beach. In December the same year the self-righting *Quiver* was taken to Halesworth and there loaded on a railway wagon to be returned to the Institution, having been on the station sixteen years and only been off once on service in very moderate weather. From first to last the men had never had confidence in her, for Southwold was one of those places on the East Anglian coast where the beachmen remained loyal to the Norfolk and Suffolk type of boat and were implacably opposed to what they termed "roly-polies." It was a carriage boat of the Norfolk and Suffolk type, named *Quiver No 2*, which came to Southwold to replace her.

The *Quiver No 2* performed several useful services during the fifteen years she was at Southwold. One of these was to the Norwegian barque *Nordhavet*, of Porzgrund, which had stranded on the shoal on 2nd May, 1887. Sam May brought nine of the crew ashore in his punt, but the captain and two mates refused to leave her. During the evening, however, it came on to blow, and at midnight the *Quiver No 2* was launched to bring the captain and the others ashore. A nameboard from the *Nordhavet* adorned one of the fishermen's sheds beside the road to the harbour until about 1970.

The *Quiver No 2* suffered damage when being launched off the carriage in a strong gale at SW on 15th August, 1890, to the assistance of the brigantine *Vectis*, of Harwich, which was in difficulties off Dunwich with her steering gear gone. The boat was thrown by the sea against the carriage and stove in four planks, as well as breaking all the spokes in one of the wheels of the carriage.

In spite of such problems the lifeboatmen succeeded in carrying the *Vectis* into Yarmouth harbour, and were awarded £70 salvage. After the accident to the carriage the *Quiver No 2* was launched off ways on the beach.

On 16th January, 1892, the *Quiver No 2* rescued the crew of four in the local punt *Mary Ann*, and then on 15th February the same year she was brought out when the schooner *Elizabeth Kilner*, of London, was observed in the bay during a strong gale at SE. Those ashore who anxiously watched her progress considered that it would be impossible for her to get off the lee shore, so horses were obtained and with the aid of the floaters on the drag ropes the lifeboat was taken through the town and up on to Easton Cliff for nearly two miles, over hedges and ditches, keeping abreast of the schooner as her captain tried desperately to claw her out of the bay.

The lifeboat had got nearly to Easton Broad when the captain of the schooner, seeing it was impossible for him to get out of the bay, put his helm up and ran the vessel straight for the lifeboat on the beach. The vessel came quite to the main and the five men on board her were got ashore by ropes, so the lifeboat was not required after all. The *Elizabeth Kilner* was sold and broken up where she lay.

In the spring of 1892 the *Coal Exchange*, quondam *Harriett*, was being swivelled on her return from an exercise when it was noticed that she set her back up and showed signs of weakness. The crew expressed their opinion that her time was up.

Her last successful service had been performed six years earlier, when on 27th December, 1886, she had been launched in a terrible gale and snowstorm which put three vessels ashore in Sizewell Bay, the schooner *Day Star*, of Ipswich, the *Magnet* and the *Trixie Wee*. John Cragie and the other lifeboatmen found the *Day Star* abreast of Sizewell Buildings and succeeded with much difficulty in rescuing four men from her. While at the wreck Cragie was again washed overboard, but his leg became entangled in some of the gear and his comrades were able to haul him on board again without damage beyond the loss of his sou'wester. The lifeboat was unable to get back to her station and had to be put ashore at Aldeburgh, being brought home three days later.

Between 1886 and 1892 the *Coal Exchange* was launched on service three times, but without result. After thirty-seven years' service, and the saving of seventy-six lives, she was condemned. She had outlasted her old coxswain by two years, for Ben Herrington "crossed the bar" in May, 1890, and was laid to rest with generations of his forefathers.

John Cragie was much involved with the design of the new boat that was to replace the *Coal Exchange*, for she was to be built by Beeching at Yarmouth to comply with the Solemen's idea of what a lifeboat should be. Of the improved Norfolk and Suffolk type, with water ballast confined in a tank, and scuppers as well as relieving valves, she was 44 feet long and 13 feet beam, rigged like the earlier boats with dipping fore-lug and standing lug mizzen.

She turned out to be the finest boat of her type ever launched, easy to float off the beach, dry and fast and as stiff as a church at sea. After nearly twenty years' service during which she performed some very heavy work she still retained the confidence and admiration of the Solemen, and if she had only been built with drop keels like some of the later boats of the same type she would have been a perfect sailing lifeboat.

The new boat was formally handed over on Easter Monday, 1893, and was christened *Alfred Corry* by Mrs. J.E. Grubbe in memory of the donor who had left funds to the Institution to establish a lifeboat. Just a hundred years later about fifty people gathered in Southwold Town Hall to celebrate with John Cragie's great-grandson, Captain John Cragie, who had spent four years restoring the *Alfred Corry* and was seeking means of ensuring the boat's survival.

The *Alfred Corry* cost £800, more than three times as much as her predecessor. Because she was somewhat larger than the *Coal Exchange* it was found necessary to enlarge the boathouse, which was done at a cost of £143.

The old *Coal Exchange* was sold to a Mr. Stephenson, of Dunwich, for

£5, and after lying on Dunwich beach for some years was again sold to Kessingland. It is to be regretted that the committee did not see their way to let her remain on the beach at Southwold for so long as she would hold together as a memorial of her long and faithful service.

The new boat was not long on her station before her services were required. On 21st November, 1893, John Cragie was informed that a vessel was drifting about in a SSE direction from the town with no sails set, and he launched at 9am in a strong gale at NE. Proceeding to the wreck, which was about eighteen miles from the land, he found she was the Norwegian barque *Alpha*, of Hermosand, loaded with wood for Seville. She had been on the Leman and Ower sands, had been abandoned by her crew, and was in tow of two fishing smacks.

The lifeboatmen assisted to get the vessel into the neighbourhood of Harwich, and then left her to fetch a tug. The barque was at last towed into Harwich about 8pm on the 22nd, and the lifeboat returned home at 4pm on the 23rd, having been absent from her station fifty-five hours. The share of salvage received by the lifeboatmen was £85.

A memorable day at Southwold was 24th October, 1894, which opened with a strong gale at S by E, with rain and a very heavy sea. At 6.30 in the morning it was reported that a vessel off Dunwich was flying signals of distress, and the *Alfred Corry* was launched at once. The lifeboat crew found that the vessel was the Norwegian barque *Nina*, of Christiania (now known as Oslo), which had been in collision.

The Dunwich self-righting lifeboat was launched about an hour after the *Alfred Corry* got off, and being closer and to windward of the vessel was able to get alongside just before the Southwold boat. Two coastguards who were in the Dunwich crew jumped on board; they found only one man in possession, a west-country fisherman who said that he had found her abandoned, had sailed as close as possible in his lugger and had jumped into the barque's rigging.

Ten Southwold men were put on board with the idea of saving the ship. They let go the anchors and commenced to stow the sails, but all in vain. She dragged in until she struck and began to break up. The Southwold lifeboat then took all the men off, including the two Dunwich coastguards who preferred not to go ashore in their own boat, and both lifeboats landed at Southwold about 3pm. The *Nina* went to the main, where she immediately broke up; her cargo of firewood strewed the shore for a couple of miles.

In the meantime those left at home had been busy, for at 12.30pm a large beach yawl was seen running past the town showing signals of distress. It was the *Courage Sans Peur*, of Lowestoft, owned by David Cook, a Lowestoft beachman who a few years later migrated to Frinton in Essex, where he carried on trade as a boatman and bathing machine proprietor.

The *Quiver No 2* was immediately launched. Her crew found the yawl unmanageable, half full of water. The five men in the yawl were taken into the lifeboat and the yawl was taken in tow to Lowestoft, where a tug took them into the harbour. The lifeboat was brought back to Southwold next morning.

When the brig *James and Eleanor*, of Shields, went ashore at Easton on 13th January, 1895, John Cragie launched the *Alfred Corry* and succeeded in reaching the wreck in half an hour. The brig's crew were in the fore rigging. The anchor was let go with a spring on the cable and the boat was veered down towards the wreck, but all at once the brig's foremast went overboard, carrying the crew with it.

One man was rescued, and the cable was then slipped. Cragie sailed the lifeboat into the raffle of rigging and rescued another man. A lifeboatman grabbed hold of a third man, but he could not break his hold on the rigging; while he was still struggling to get him aboard the grapnel which one of the crew had thrown into the rigging gave way and the lifeboat was driven broadside on to the beach.

Two other men were washed ashore alive, and three Southwold men later received medals for rescuing them at the risk of their own lives, but the captain and two others were lost that dreadful morning. John Cragie took the hat round and put up a stone to their memory in the corner of Sole churchyard where the drowned sailormen lie.

The lifeboatmen were loud in their praise of the new boat, and but for the tremendous sea pulling the arm of the grapnel out straight it is probable the other men would have been saved. So heavy was the sea that by nine o'clock that morning the brig was all to matchwood and her planking was washing along in front of the town.

The 1890s proved to be a stormy decade, and there was plenty of work for John Cragie and his men. The ketch *Eliza and Alice*, a billyboy built at Leeds in 1866, was caught riding in the bay on 25th September, 1896, with a whole gale from the south, and as she was in a very dangerous position it was decided to launch the *Alfred Corry*. She was got off through a very heavy sea after several attempts and remained by the vessel in case she was needed, but the wind drew more alongshore and the ketch's crew were able to get the anchors and sail clear of the land.

That proved to be John Cragie's last service in the lifeboat, and on 31st March, 1898, he retired. He was presented by Captain Holmes, the Inspector of Lifeboats, with the Institution's third service clasp and a certificate of service recording his faithful service in the lifeboats over fifty years, entitling him to a pension of £12 a year. He had been second coxswain for twenty-one years and coxswain for nineteen .

Fearless, capable and resolute, he was a fine specimen of the old-time longshoreman. During part of his time he had a peppery, voluble old Irishman to deal with as secretary. One day the secretary got into a tantrum over some small matter, and having blown off enough to have exasperated most men, finished by saying, "But there, John, never mind what I say; you know what I am, don't you?"

"Yes sir, I know what you are, right well I do, but I don't like it none the more for that," quietly replied long-suffering old John.

Two more utterly different dispositions could hardly be found, but when John Cragie died in November, 1903, that venerable old Hibernian was one of his most sincere mourners. Presently, after lifelong service in the Navy and for the lifeboat, we carried him to his rest in the same churchyard. Their work was done, and done well.

3 Skipper Whyard and Captain Pattman

IN SAM WHYARD, of Orford, smackmaster, and Robert Pattman, of Southwold, master mariner, we have men of a rather different type, one a deep-sea fisherman working the bleak North Sea and the other a captain of deepwater ships rolling around the Seven Seas of the world.

Of Samuel Whyard I know but little, except that he hailed from that old, old Suffolk port of Orford, once the home of many of his kind, and that he was master of the smack *Jemima*, of Woodbridge Port, a cutter-rigged vessel of twenty-eight tons built at Brittlesea, or Brightlingsea as we call it today, as far back as 1809. She was owned by Henry Whyard, of Orford, and carried a crew of seven. I have a note that in 1861 she was a pilot cutter on the Aldeburgh station, but by 1876 she was a fishing smack.

The normal job of Skipper Whyard and his crew would be trawling, or codding, in home waters and in the North Sea, according to the season. The fishing was varied by a bit of what was called hereabouts "saltwagering", that is, assisting vessels in trouble among the numerous and dangerous sands of the Thames Estuary and salving cargo and gear from wrecks.

In the nineteenth century lots of these little craft, known like their crews as "Swin Rangers", knocked about among the sands in bad weather looking out for a job, and the Customs received many complaints about smacksmen pillaging wrecks and reporting only a small proportion of the stuff they saved, the rest being smuggled ashore and sold on the quiet. A favourite dodge was to pass the material from smack to smack far out at sea; goods salved off Harwich would be taken into Ramsgate or Brightlingsea by smacks returning home from a legitimate fishing trip with a catch for sale.

The life was rough and tough, and the earnings a continual gamble. The men had to be hard as nails, and some were no doubt next door to pirates. A good yarn is told at Southwold of one of the longshore variety of semi-pirate. One fine day a Dutch bom, one of those strange-looking herring drifters built to work off the beaches at Scheveningen and elsewhere on the coast of South Holland, sailed ashore on Southwold beach for water and grub, in accordance with their custom at home. A fisherman baiting his lines nearby saw the chance of a lifetime, rushed down, climbed on board and proceeded to take charge. Mynheer Kapitan objected strongly. "Yah, yah," he began. "Yah yah be damned," said our worthy, "I'm the fust man aboard o' this wassel and she's mine!" And the Dutchmen had quite a job to get rid of him. Whether this little story is gospel or merely pub gossip not all the wise men of the East could settle now.

All the same for that, there were men among these Saltwagerers of fine character and indomitable courage, as the following simple narrative of a typical wreck will amply prove. During a dreadful gale from the east with snow on 7th January, 1876, the Norwegian barque *Hunter*, of Krageroe, laden with hop poles, went aground on the middle of the Shipwash Sand during the night. The *Jemima* was dodging under the lee of the sand, and at 7.30am Whyard saw the ship and went as near as possible, but could not get to her for broken water. While Whyard and his crew were lying there the barque's main and mizzen masts went over, but they could see the crew were in the roundhouse, and they signalled to them that they were seen.

Whyard kept as near as possible to leeward, so that if she broke up he might be able to rescue the people. At five o'clock, coming dark, he put the helm hard up and ran into Harwich, went ashore and reported to the Customs and Lloyd's agent, then went to the tug *Liverpool* and arranged to meet her at the wreck at daylight. The *Jemima* got under way again at 9.30pm and they spent the night slogging to windward against that perishing winter gale, arriving near the wreck at four o'clock next morning. There they waited for daylight, tacking to and fro between the Bawdsey and Shipwash sands, with broken water on either hand, in their sixty-seven-year-old packet, which must have gone to pieces like an orange box if she had touched on either of those cruel, hungry sands.

Only those who have beaten out of Harwich against a strong nor'easter in a sailing craft, and been almost surrounded by broken water, can really appreciate the conditions under which those gallant smacksmen, with very little prospect of any reward, lay by the *Hunter* on the chance of being able to save the crew when she broke up, showing flares from time to time to encourage them to hang on. Some of my older readers will have had some, as well as the writer.

By the courtesy of Dr. J.L. Groom, of Woodbridge, who has an old Harwich letterbook, I am able to give the rest of this story in the words of the chief characters concerned. Captain John Carrington of the tug *Liverpool* stated that he left Harwich at 11.14pm and arrived at the Shipwash at 12.30am on 8th January, but could not find the wreck. They did, however, fall in with a French schooner in a sinking state, put four men aboard and towed her to Harwich, losing the small boat on the job. After getting another boat, Captain Carrington left again for the Shipwash at 4.30am, and he reported:

> Saw the wreck of a three-masted vessel, with foremast standing, about one and a half miles from Swatchway Buoy. Saw the crew on top of deckhouse waving their hands; made towards them several times, but could not reach them for broken water and wreckage. Saw vessel breaking up fast. About 8am went in boat as near as could be and hove a line on board, and eight hands were hauled through the water into the boat; the captain jumped overboard and swam to the boat, and was taken in. Then took them aboard tug, gave them some provisions and made for Harwich; landed there about 11am.

The *Liverpool* was a clinker-built wooden paddle tug of 116 tons, built in 1870 and owned by W.J. Watts, of Harwich; she was licensed to carry ninety passengers. Only weeks before the wreck of the *Hunter* she had done fine work at the wreck of the Hamburg-Amerika liner *Deutschland* on the Kentish Knock, when she rescued no fewer than 173 people. I was amused to read in an account of these old Tyne-built paddle tugs in *Smith's Dock Journal* in 1933 of one named *Henry Clasper* which carried an organ played by the wind as she steamed along; it would have played "Hell's Bells" that night in '76.

The statement of C.B. Neilsen, master of the *Hunter*, was matter-of-fact, yet full of gratitude to the men of the *Jemima*:

> The smack *Jemima* lay by us as close as possible during a strong gale, with snow squalls and heavy sea, from 8am on 7th, till dusk. We saw her again at daybreak on the 8th, lying to as close as she could get, and about an hour after the *Liverpool* came up, and as soon as my vessel broke up the deckhouse drifted off the sand, and they got all hands in the boat and took us to the tug. We saw several smacks not far off, but the *Jemima* only kept by us, and it was owing to the confidence with which this inspired us, and to the fact, which I afterwards learned, that she went during the night, during the heavy gale, to Harwich and got the tug, that our lives were saved.

To close this graphic story of steadfast heroism, I will quote from the *Lifeboat Journal* for May, 1876:

> Feb. 3: Voted the Silver Medal of the Institution and £5 to Mr. John Carrington, Master of the steam tug *Liverpool*, of Harwich, and £9 to four other men for putting off in a boat from the tug and saving the crew of nine men from the Norwegian barque *Hunter*, of Krageroe, which was wrecked on the Shipwash Sands during an Easterly gale on the 7th January. £10 were also granted to the other ten men forming the crew of the tug.
>
> Also £10 to Mr. Samuel Whyard, Master of the smack *Jemima*, of Orford, and his crew of six men, in acknowledgement of their laudable services on the occasion of the wreck of the *Hunter*.

It will be observed that the *Liverpool's* people collected the lion's whack, in accordance with the custom of the service, they being the actual salvors; but all will agree that Skipper Whyard and his crew were the undoubted heroes of the piece, and Orford folk may well be proud of the part played by their townsmen in this thrilling drama off their stormy old Orford Ness.

With regard to this little story of the sea, an unknown friend who signed himself "Raydon Point" wrote me such an interesting letter that I make bold to give it here, perforce without permission, at the same time thanking him for his personal memory of this old sea-warrior and his sad fate, explaining why I was unable to find any stone to him in Orford churchyard:

> I am a native of Orford (although away for over thirty years) and as a lad I well remember Captain Whyard. When I first knew him he came home from sea and retired for a time. He was a broad-shouldered, powerful old man, clean shaven except for side-whiskers; just the sort one might have imagined Captain Cuttle to be.
>
> I remember him so well because he used to attend morning service at Orford Church and sat just in front of my family. On Sundays he wore a well-kept top hat, such as I am told the old-time skippers used to carry when they went ashore on business.
>
> In those days he owned the schooner *Ariel*, and employed a skipper to run her. But I suppose times were not too good and after a while he took her over again, and used to bring cargoes of coal from the north and sell at Orford. On his last voyage he had with him a mate from Woodbridge and two Orford men as his third and fourth hands.

He came out of Seaham (I think it was) into that terrible gale of November, 1893, and vanished; nothing was ever seen or heard either of ship or crew. This tragedy made a deep impression upon me, and to this day when I hear the wintry gale I wonder what was the end of poor old Sam Whyard and his crew, and in particular the third hand, Edward Barham, with whom I had many yarns and held in great esteem.

A kindly tribute from a generous spirit which adds considerably to the interest of my tale.

* * *

In the fifties and sixties of last century a Robert Pattman, shoemaker, lived by Bank Alley in Southwold High Street, being sometime an Overseer of the Borough, and there his son Bob was born at a time when Southwold was a busy little coasting and fishing port, with a wonderful prospect of the shipping of the world passing up and down or sheltering in the often-crowded anchorage in Solebay.

The bleak but invigorating Suffolk coast has produced many fine seamen, with centuries of seafaring traditions behind them, but for want of local opportunities any who wanted to get on in the shipping world had to range far from home. That was the case with young Pattman, who as soon as schooling was done in 1864 shipped as boy aboard the *Woodland Lass*, 120 tons, of Southwold, in which he made a voyage to the north and back. Then he shifted to the *Heart of Oak*, also hailing from Southwold, for a trip down to Hartlepool for coals.

These little vessels were square rigged forward, like a topsail schooner, but had a ketch's mizzen, and so were dubbed "jackass schooners". I remember the old *Heart of Oak* as one of those which would go a long way in a long time. She had been built at Southwold in 1836, and after fifty years' faithful service was broken up there about the time of Queen Victoria's Golden Jubilee. Between 1860 and 1870 she belonged to Joseph Dix, of Dunwich, and used to run on the beach there in the summer to discharge coals. It was just as well she was *Heart of Oak*.

The *Woodland Lass* had been built at Lowestoft in 1851 and was owned by Edward Chapman, of Southwold. I have been told that she was the last one to go up to Blythburgh Bridge with timber. She was wrecked at Sizewell Sluice some time in the eighties. Pattman then made a voyage to

A billyboy, possibly the *Woodland Lass*, in Southwold harbour. She sets square topsails on the foremast, and is what was dubbed by contemporary seamen a "jackass schooner".

Russia as apprentice in the barque *Advice*, but he received such cruel treatment that on his return his father prosecuted both captain and mate. The former received eighteen months and the mate three years, both of them with hard labour, and the indentures were cancelled.

This would have choked most boys off the sea, but the boy Bob straightaway made another trip down north in the *Heart of Oak*, and then spent a year in the *Hubertus*, a real old-time Geordie collier brig. In her he voyaged to London, Hamburg, Boulogne and Dieppe carrying coal from Seaham. Her skipper could neither read nor write, and Bob acted as his clerk as well as serving as ordinary seaman.

After that he served twelve years in all sorts of sailing ships, voyaging to all parts of the world, to Aden, India, China and Australia. He went through all the ratings from ordinary seaman to master, reaping his well-won reward in 1879 when he was appointed captain of R. & J. Craig's full-rigged ship *County of Bute* and started on his long and successful career in command of clipper ships in the colonial trade.

A couple of voyages to the East followed in the same owner's four-poster *County of Selkirk*, and then at the end of 1882 he was offered the command of the famous *Loch Torridon* on her second voyage. This celebrated clipper, owned by Aitken & Lilburn of Glasgow, was an iron four-masted barque of 2,000 tons register carrying well over 4,000 tons of cargo, and was considered by Sir G.M. White, the Admiralty naval architect, one of the most graceful and elegant models ever built in the Glasgow yards. Notwithstanding her size, Captain Pattman said the smallest boy on board could steer her even in the worst of weather, thanks to perfect sparring. To which I would add, thanks also to his judicious sail carrying, which made this *Loch* one of the favourite passenger ships running from Glasgow to Australia and carried her through many a heavy gale in the Atlantic, off the Horn, and down under in the Roaring Forties, where in 1893 they fell in with ice 1,500 feet high.

In 1892 there were seventy-seven of the world's finest sailing ships loading wool in Australia, and the *Loch Torridon* beat the lot that year—eighty-one days, Sydney to the Lizard, and only two days more to dock.

Many men who rose to command their own ships owed much to Captain Pattman, who took a good deal of trouble over the training of his apprentices, as Basil Lubbock records in his book *The Colonial Clippers*, in which he tells at length the life stories both of this splendid ship and of her Suffolk master. He has kindly given me leave to quote him and to reproduce both ship and captain.

I must be content to say here that Captain Pattman commanded the *Loch Torridon* for twenty-six years without a break, and without any very serious casualty. He only left her in 1908 on account of the difficulty of getting really good crews. He then went into steam.

In 1912, when his ship was butting into a gale Land's End way, a huge sea broke over the bridge and badly fractured one of his legs. They put this great seaman ashore at Falmouth, and there he died in hospital.

At least he was spared the pain of learning of his old ship's miserable fate. She was sold that year to the Russians, and one can imagine the slovenly state into which she quickly dropped. Many little Russian ships used to trade to Yarmouth, and as a boy I used to declare that I could tell a Russian, without looking, by the stink. In January, 1915, the old *Loch Torridon* was dismasted down channel, the Russian crew were taken out by the British steamer *Orduna*, and that one-time queen of the ocean was abandoned, derelict and filling fast.

* * *

Here, then, is a brief account of two old-time Suffolk storm warriors, one from each end of the ladder, showing the stuff of which they were made in the days of sail.

James Cable, who first went to sea in cod smacks and became coxswain of the Aldeburgh lifeboat in 1888, at the helm of the *City of Winchester*

4 James Cable

THE CABLE family have been well-known Suffolk seafarers for centuries; perhaps their calling gave them their very appropriate surname. John Cable was master of the *Handmayde*, of Ipswich, employed in the coal trade to London, in 1636.

Nearly two centuries later there was a William Cable at Aldeburgh, and the 1844 directory gives Charles, two Johns, Thomas and another William, a pilot. James, the subject of this memoir, was born 13th December, 1851, the grandson of Thomas, drowned when the Aldeburgh lifeboat capsized in 1859, and son of Thomas, an acting coastguard, who was drowned in 1855 swimming off to the brig *Vesta* with a line by which seven of her crew were saved. After the seven had been hauled ashore the line broke, and Cable and two others of the crew were lost. On that dreadful day forty sail were driving ashore on the Suffolk coast.

Before he was fourteen young Cable started his sea days in one of the Aldeburgh cod smacks, similar to Whyard's *Jemima* but rather larger, and served in the codbangers for five or six years, from cabin boy at 2s.6d. (12p) to full man at £1 a week. They worked as far north as the Orkneys and Faeroes, and in the summer months went to Norway for lobsters. It was a hard life, as I have said before, and it is good to have a first-hand account of this long deceased phase of deep-sea fishing in the little book, *A Lifeboatman's Days, Told by Himself*, which he wrote in his retirement.

The fish were caught on hand-lines worked over the smack's rail or on long-lines worked from a small boat. The cod were kept alive in the well, which was full of holes so that seawater circulated around it. When there was a large catch the cod were split and salted and packed into the hold.

In 1871 he felt the East a-calling and made a couple of voyages to Penang and Singapore in small barques in which the grub appears to

51

have been very bad, nothing but salt beef, salt pork, and rice once a week. Then he shipped for Australia in the auxiliary passenger ship *Duke of Northumberland*, an iron vessel of 558 tons. After three months at home in Aldeburgh he and some friends joined the same ship for another voyage to Melbourne, and on arrival there Cable went up country to visit an uncle, finding him still talking good, broad Suffolk. There he spent a considerable time, and he has left us a good description of life on a sheep station and in the bush in the eighteen-eighties.

Home once more, now a capable and experienced sailorman, Cable put in a couple of seasons yachting. Strangely enough, his first berth was in the *Rescue*, Joshua Chard's presentation lifeboat, which had been converted to a yacht. They put into Calais, and there she sat on a pile which came up through the bottom of the boat; the owner, running short of cash, raised money on the boat to pay their passages home—and that was that.

In 1879 Cable bought some bathing machines and fishing boats and settled down at Aldeburgh for good, to his mother's relief; on his return from Australia she had begged him not to go long voyages again. The following year he was appointed second coxswain of the Aldeburgh lifeboat *George Hounsfield*, a self-righter which had been built by Forrestt at Limehouse in 1870 and served at Aldeburgh for twenty years. When replaced in 1890 by the *Aldeburgh* she remained on the beach close to Cable's bathing machines.

Of James Cable's very many services in the Aldeburgh boats there is only space to mention a few of the principal and most successful efforts. His first launch as second coxswain was on 6th January, 1881, when they went thirty miles in a great gale on a fruitless errand to the ill-fated *Indian Chief* on the Longsand. The Ramsgate boat, towed by the tug *Vulcan*, had already saved the survivors, earning undying fame for the Ramsgate men.

At that time messages as to ships in distress were sent from the Sunk lightship and other lightvessels to Harwich by pigeon; had the news been passed on to Aldeburgh when it was received on 5th January it is likely that the Aldeburgh boat would have been first on the scene, as the Harwich lifeboatmen were let down by the owner of the tug that took them out and the Ramsgate men had a very long tow.

On 16th October, 1881, the Aldeburgh men salved the schooner *Equity*, of Boston, and saved the crew, including the captain's wife, taking them safely into Harwich. And on 6th October the following year, after great difficulties, the lifeboat rescued most of the crew of the schooner *Rambler*, which had entirely disappeared before the boat got back to her berth.

In 1888 Cable was promoted coxswain. Soon afterwards he had three calls in one week, saving fifteen from the steamer *Sirius* and also the crew of a Norwegian timber vessel; but the crew of a third wreck had left in their own boat before the lifeboat arrived. All these wrecks occurred in the vicinity of Thorpeness. Reference to the Wreck Chart published in 1874 shows that there were more wrecks between Cromer and the South Foreland than anywhere else in the United Kingdom, the Suffolk coast providing a considerable proportion. Statistical records show that for the period of five years ending 1871 there were 9,028 casualties, an annual average of 1,805, and one can understand that lifeboats and shipbuilders were kept busy.

On 1st November, 1890, the *George Hounsfield* salved a schooner from the Shipwash and took her to Harwich. That was her last service in humanity's cause. The next boat, named *Aldeburgh*, was built at Yarmouth by J.H. Critten to the ideas of her coxswain and crew, and while she was building Cable was acting as one of the judges at the lifeboat trials held at Lowestoft in January, February and March, 1891.

Having assisted two small yachts from Woodbridge in August, the *Aldeburgh's* first good service was on 11th November, 1891, when she rescued sixteen of the crew and a Trinity pilot from the Norwegian barque *Winifred*, dismasted during a heavy gale. Cable narrates how he took the boat under the bowsprit so that the men could slide down a rope, the most awkward to save being the pilot, a Southwold man, who would bring his bag with him. This caused him to slip down headfirst into the sea, and they pulled him on board by the legs. I remember seeing Pilot Claxton land from the Southwold train on his return, still hanging on to that precious bag. Cable does not mention it, but both he and second coxswain William Mann received the RNLI silver medal for this fine and successful service.

In 1892 they rescued two more vessels from the Shipwash graveyard, and a four-masted barque from Thorpeness, and on 25th October Cable and his willing crew made another great rescue from a vessel on the Longsand or the Kentish Knock, thirty or forty miles from home. The crew were in the rigging, one man with a broken leg, so Charles Ward had to go up and lower him down. With the help of a lucky tow they were able to make Harwich.

About this time Cable was awarded the Royal Humane Society's medal and two certificates for rescuing bathers in trouble, and soon afterwards he received a large engraved silver cup from the Finnish Consul for a great rescue from a dismasted and waterlogged vessel, the barque *Venscapen*, wrecked off the town on 20th November, 1893. This vessel was seen at daylight driving ashore, a hapless wreck, with masts gone and the crew lashed to the stump of the foremast.

The *Aldeburgh* was launched in the teeth of a tremendous sea and anchored in such a position that the ship drove down upon her. The instant they came together the cable was cut with a hatchet and ship and lifeboat drifted alongside while the crew were taken out with all haste, for the deadly inner shoal was close under the lee, potential death to all hands.

Cable got clear of the wreck a few minutes before she struck and started to break up, and in view of the raging sea on the beach he decided to run for Harwich. While passing through Hollesley Bay the lifeboatmen saw a vessel flying signals of distress; they found her to be the Hull pilot cutter *Fox*, with eight men aboard, driven from the Humber, clean swept, sails gone and pumps choked.

Two lifeboatmen jumped on board and, escorted by the *Aldeburgh*, she was navigated safely into Harwich, where they landed the *Venscapen's* crew. The lifeboatmen were being well looked after ashore when a message came that the Shipwash light was firing, so off went Cable and his crew again and thrashed their boat some eight or ten miles out to the Shipwash Sand, to find only a mass of wreckage, all that was left of a fine ship that had broken up while they were fighting the gale to get there.

Then back again to Harwich about midnight, to spend the rest of the night ashore after a long and trying service which Cable always declared was the best bit of lifeboat work ever done at Aldeburgh. It was effected in full view of the town; a fine picture of the rescue of the *Venscapen's* crew was painted by an Aldeburgh artist, R. Andre, who was there on the beach. A very good reproduction is given at page 283 of Patterson's *A Hero of the Sea*, the life story of Lieutenant J.O. Williams, RN, who was for many years the highly efficient hon. secretary of the Aldeburgh lifeboats and contributed not a little to their many successful services. Lieutenant Williams, late District Officer of the Coastguard, died at Aldeburgh on 30th December, 1925, aged eighty-two, a real storm warrior respected by all along the Suffolk coast, although he was a "foreigner", hailing from far Pembroke, and had up to 1890 spent all his life in revenue cutters and on the west coast. There he earned the RNLI silver medal and second service clasp for gallantry in saving life.

Cable was on the sick list when the *Aldeburgh*, having already been launched on service fifty-four times and having saved 152 lives, was launched into a raging sea on 7th December, 1899. Although he was suffering from influenza Cable donned his oilskins and went down to the beach, but the local doctor saw him as he was about to put on a lifebelt and forbade him to go. Charles Ward, a former coxswain and then bowman of the lifeboat, took command.

The boat was launched and sailed to the southward with the flood tide, but as she was crossing the shoal two or three heavy waves broke into the boat, another mighty wave crashed on board, and she turned over on her side. Then as the masts touched the ground they broke off, and she turned bottom up, trapping six of the lifeboatmen.

When she came ashore bottom up Cable got on to the boat and tried to hack through the bottom with an axe, but after cutting through the planking there were air cases and deck to get through, and he could not do it. About two hundred helpers tried to lift the boat with long poles, but

The overturned lifeboat *Aldeburgh* after the disaster of 7th December, 1899, in which six men died. The hole which Coxswain Cable cut with an axe in a vain rescue attempt can be seen clearly.

only when the tide went down could men crawl under the boat to where the six were trapped.

Six men died that day, and another died later from the effects of the disaster. Cable himself got wet through twice that day, and most of his friends thought he would die of the cold. But his wife had plenty of hot water and mustard ready for him when he returned home, and he recovered after a few days.

Cable's many services in the *Reserve No 1*, the former Winterton lifeboat *Margaret* which was brought to Aldeburgh to replace the ill-fated *Aldeburgh*, the *City of Winchester* and the No 2 boat *Edward Z. Dresden*, and the splendid record of the station during the whole of this time, is set out on the service boards on Aldeburgh front.

The Aldeburgh No. 1 lifeboat *City of Winchester*, built by Thames Iron Works as a replacement for the *Aldeburgh* after the 1899 disaster. She was reckoned by the Aldeburgh men to be the finest Norfolk and Suffolk class type boat ever built.

The writer had the honour to take part in the procession when the *City of Winchester* was named in 1904 and also to be present by invitation at the christening of the *Abdy Beauclerk*, Aldeburgh's first motor lifeboat, in 1931. Built by Thames Iron Works at a cost of £2,640, the *City of Winchester* was regarded by the Aldeburgh men as the finest Norfolk and Suffolk type boat

ever built; she spent twenty-six years at Aldeburgh, and finished her life as a houseboat on the River Blackwater at Maldon.

I also met Cable and his crew at sea when the "Navvy" (General Steam Navigation Company) boat *Plover* was ashore at Misner before the First World War. I hailed the coxswain to come aboard the tug, and had a long mardle while waiting for high water. "The man's mad," said Cable, "won't take any assistance

Left: Launching the *City of Winchester* to the aid of a barge on 6th March, 1913.

Below: The two lifeboats, the *Edward Z. Dresden* on its carriage in the foreground and the *City of Winchester* in the near distance, on Aldeburgh beach about 1910.

and the flood nearly done." But the captain was not so barmy as he thought, for after a tedious wait, rolling about in the perishing cold, the steamboat backed off unaided and went her way without saying "thank you."

"There goes my wife's new bonnet," said the engineer. "Pull up the hook," said the tug captain. "So long, coxswain," and lifeboat and tug parted, homeward bound. Another blank!

During that war there were many risky and troublesome jobs, and life on the coast was full of anxieties which left their mark on those who went through it, including our coxswain. Feeling the effects of wartime worries and Anno Domini, he retired in 1917, full of years and honours. To the latter were then added a certificate of service, £50 and a pension, besides which his portrait was painted and hangs in the historic Moot Hall at the back of Aldeburgh beach.

On 22nd May, 1930, Cable had a stroke while working on his boat by the sea, on which so much of his life had been spent. He died that afternoon, and on 27th May, with many of his shipmates and the borough dignitaries, I followed him to his last berth amid the respect of the whole town, and now am spared to write this inadequate tribute to my friend, the man who kept no count of the lives he saved.

*   *   *

The Aldeburgh station received a new lifeboat, a self-righting motor lifeboat of the Rother class, from the Sussex boatyard of William Osborne in 1982. At a ceremony on 20th September of that year the Duke of Kent named the new boat *RNLB James Cable*, in honour of the man who was coxswain for twenty-nine eventful years.

5 Samuel Charles May

On foreign seas he fell but not by storm
Which boisterous winds the heaving seas deform.
Nor by the Rock beneath the Tide concealed,
Nor by the sword which warring nations wield,
But by the foe received in friendship's guise,
By hands of treacherous Pirates lo he dies.

THESE LINES are on a stone by Southwold Church gate (where lie so many of the May family) erected to the memory of David May, who lost his life in the Gulf of Florida on 28th June, 1819, on board the West Indiaman *Ann*. The story of that act of piracy cannot be recovered now, but Sam May used to say that his great-uncle's tongue was cut out before they finished him off, so I suspect David ticked the pirates off properly for their treachery.

I introduce this to develop my theme of the great story, as yet but half told, of the widespread services of Suffolk men in the English sea affair. That this spirit still flourishes in families is proved by the fact that Sam May's own nephew had his ship sunk under him while serving as gunner in a merchant steamer and spent some days as a prisoner on board a German submarine during the First World War.

For a good part of our lives Sam May and I were on terms of close friendship, and I knew him, his fine qualities and his quaint ways, so well, in both fair weather and foul, that I may perhaps have some difficulty in seeing the wood for the trees. However, no account of the Suffolk Storm Warriors would be complete without him.

Samuel Charles May was born in Southwold in 1860, son of James May, who met the headless woman on the Gunhill the day he and John Hurr rescued Robert English after his twin boys had already been drowned. He

spent his boyhood with other young tigers ranging about among the boats on the beach, so of course nothing would stop him from "following the water," as people used to call it then. Some fishing voyages were made in the little "half and halfers" out of Southwold, and then he married and settled down to longshoring.

One of an earlier generation was wont to complain that the rising crowd were not half so enterprising as in his young time. "I'll tell you how it is now," he would say, "fust they get a shrimp bote, then they get a trawl bote, and then they get married and then they're done." Sam was by no means done, for no man led a more active and industrious life than he.

Samuel May, who became second coxswain of the Southwold lifeboats in 1891 and was elected coxswain in succession to John Craigie in 1898.

By the time he was thirty May was a recognised leader on the beach. I have no note of his first trip in the lifeboat, but on 2nd May, 1887, May brought ashore in his punt nine of the crew of the Norwegian barque *Nordhavet*, of Porsgrund, and I have no doubt he was in the *Quiver No 2* when she floated that night and saved the captain and mates who had refused to leave when he landed the other nine men.

In 1891 Sam was appointed second coxswain of the *Coal Exchange*, formerly the *Harriett*, which was then nearing the end of her thirty-seven years on station. Southwold then being a two-boat station, he occupied the same position in the *Quiver No 2*, a carriage boat.

With John Cragie he was chiefly responsible for the planning of the *Alfred Corry*, which was built in 1893. During the whole of May's service

60

of twenty-seven years he never failed to get the lifeboats afloat, no matter what the weather was, and I do not think that he was excelled by any man in the difficult feat of floating from such an exposed beach. At any rate in 1896 the Institution selected Southwold for the German Chief Inspector of Lifeboats to witness a launch from the open beach, and he reported that he was much impressed by the power of the *Alfred Corry* and the capable manner in which she was worked.

May's first service as second coxswain was to the Norwegian barque *Alpha* on 21st November, 1893, and the following year he was in the launch to the barque *Nina*, and also that to the *James and Eleanor*, when two men were saved. Then, on 27th January, 1898, he was elected coxswain, and I believe that during her twenty-five years' duty the *Alfred Corry* was never afloat on service without him, and they never let each other down.

The *Alfred Corry* was launched in the same gale in which the Aldeburgh lifeboat was capsized with the loss of seven of her crew. The news of this terrible accident made a great sensation in Southwold, but when just before midnight information was received of a ship aground on the Shipwash there was no hanging back on the part of the Southwold men. In the *Alfred Corry* they searched the whole length of the Shipwash all night without finding anything. At daybreak a steamer was discovered at anchor, apparently unmanageable. Although no reply could be got from her, the lifeboatmen were in no doubt that she had been on the sand in the night and had been fortunate enough to get off.

This is an instance of the many cases in which ships get into difficulties and signal for assistance, but afterwards succeed in getting clear. In the meantime perhaps two lifeboats have been launched and have been knocking about all night in fearful weather; when they find the casualty the lifeboatmen are told they are not wanted or, as in this case, cannot even get a reply from the vessel that a few hours earlier was so anxious for assistance.

Later that same month, at daybreak on the 28th, the Harwich brigantine *Economy* was seen trying to beat out of the bay in a strong gale at south-east by south. She tacked off Dunwich and was going off to sea well when about eleven o'clock her foretopmast carried away and she began to drive rapidly to leeward. The *Alfred Corry* was quickly launched to her assistance, and getting a rope aboard Sam May endeavoured to save the vessel.

The rope broke, however, and as the *Economy* seemed doomed to go ashore Coxswain May took the crew off, with great difficulty. The *Economy*, an old vessel built at Sunderland in 1848 and owned at the time of her loss by William Reason of Manningtree, drove ashore at Covehithe Ness and became a total wreck in a very short time.

In 1897 the *Quiver No 2* was condemned and returned to London. To take her place a new boat of the Norfolk and Suffolk type, 32ft long and 9ft beam, was built at Lowestoft by Henry Reynolds out of funds provided under the will of Mr. J.B. Barkworth, the brother of a former member of the Southwold committee. May and the other lifeboatmen were consulted when the new boat, which was exhibited by the RNLI at the Jubilee Exhibition in London in 1897, was being designed.

She was christened *Rescue* by Mrs. Barkworth on 7th September, 1897, but it was several years before she performed her first service. That came on 9th June, 1904, when she was launched about 11pm to the assistance of three men in the local punt *Rapid*; it was 2.30 the next morning before the lifeboatmen could find the little boat and rescue her occupants.

Lifeboat work was anything but regular, and while the *Rescue* was not called upon for several years the *Alfred Corry* was called out on fruitless errands on 12th November, 1901, and 3rd December, 1902.

In 1904 the sea attacked the lifeboat houses at Southwold, undermining the front of the buildings, and the *Alfred Corry* had to be taken out. The Institution close-piled the front at a cost of £160, and this, together with the extension of the harbour piers in 1907, saved the houses from a similar fate to that of the old house under North Cliff.

At daylight on 27th November, 1905, the Coastguard reported to Sam May that something was ashore at Covehithe, and as soon as it was light enough the masts of a sunken vessel could be seen with a glass. The *Alfred Corry* was launched at 7.30am, the wind then being WSW, a moderate gale and sea after a heavy gale at SSW most of the night. The wreck was reached at 8am, when it was seen to be a smack with the crew hanging on to the foremasthead in the greatest peril as the vessel rolled from side to side in the swell. The cries of these poor fellows as the lifeboat approached were most piteous, and Coxswain May lost not a moment in laying the lifeboat alongside the mast.

Three men dropped into the boat without difficulty, but a boy was astride the forestay, and it was evident he had been there so long he could not move. One of the lifeboatmen had to go up and help him down. Some of the rescued men were only partly dressed, as they had turned out when she struck, and they had suffered much from exposure in their desperate position. The Covehithe rocket brigade had got a line fast and had saved a lad, but the apparatus got foul and they could not work it again.

The smack was the French trawler *Joseph et Yvonne*, of Dunquerque, which had struck on the Barber about four o'clock in the morning and had sunk in deep water inside the sand. The lifeboat was towed back to Southwold by the tug *Lowestoft* and

This photograph of the crew of the French trawler *Joseph et Yvonne* was taken by E.R.Cooper as the lifeboat *Alfred Corry* approached the wreck.

landed the men about 9am, having been gone only an hour and a half. Three years later the French government awarded silver medals and diplomas to the two coxswains and the secretary, who on this occasion had gone in the lifeboat, and bronze medals and diplomas to the rest of the crew in respect of this service, the awards being presented at a public meeting on 29th October, 1908.

In the summer of 1906 the Belgian smack *Rosaline-Fidoline*, of Ostend, was burnt at sea somewhere abreast of Southwold; the crew took to the boat and were picked up next morning by two Southwold fishermen out trawling. The men were brought ashore at Southwold and taken to the agent of the Shipwrecked Mariners Society, who immediately recognised one man as a member of the crew of the *Joseph et Yvonne*. The man made signs that he wanted new clothing, but the agent said "No, my boy, you are dry this time, and you don't get another rig-out quite so soon."

That same year, 1906, the Institution sent down a set of experimental lifebelts constructed of kapok, a cotton-like substance which is obtained from the seed pods of the *Eriodendron Anfractuosum*, from the Malay peninsula. Sam May and the men approved of the new lifebelts, which were more bouyant than the old cork belts, as well as warmer and much more comfortable, and a favourable report was sent up to headquarters. Kapok belts entered general use, and before long the familiar cork belts disappeared from the lifeboat service.

Several vessels anchored in the bay for shelter from a northerly gale on 31st January, 1907, and a steamboat that turned out to be the *Cedric*, of Landskrona, was observed making signals for a doctor and reporting an accident. As there was too much swell for a shore boat to go off, the *Rescue* was launched with Dr. Basil Tripp and the secretary on board. Dr. Tripp, who lived at the Manor House in Southwold High Street, was medical officer of health to the Corporation and surgeon to both the Admiralty and Trinity House as well as being a local GP.

When Sam May brought the lifeboat alongside the Swedish steamer it was found that a Russian Finn named Arthur Johansen had crushed his hand in the steam windlass two days before; inspection revealed a terrible wound which must have caused him intense agony. We took him ashore and to the hospital, where he remained for many months. First part of his hand, then the whole hand, and eventually part of his arm had to be amputated because the wound had been so long neglected.

During a blowing night on 13th December, 1907, a flare was seen opposite the town about 11pm and the *Alfred Corry* was quickly launched. Sam May found that the vessel was the spritsail barge *Decima*, of London, one of E.J. & W. Goldsmith's big steel barges, built at Southampton in 1899. Her topmast and sprit had carried away, and all her sails were gone.

In going alongside the lifeboat was thrown by a heavy sea against the barge's leeboard and considerably damaged. The two men on the *Decima* refused to come out, as the vessel was not making water, and the captain engaged the lifeboatmen to get him a tug. Coxswain May therefore set sail for Lowestoft, the crew of the barge letting go their anchor about three or four miles from the shore. The lifeboat reached Lowestoft at 3am and left soon afterwards in tow of the paddle tug *Despatch*. The towrope broke

The Southwold No 2 boat *Rescue* putting a doctor on board the Swedish steamer *Cedric* in a northerly gale to attend a seaman whose hand had been crushed in the steam windlass two days earlier.

once as the heavy sea imposed an impossible strain, but a new rope was hauled aboard and the search for the *Decima* went on.

At last the barge was discovered about nine miles from the land; she had been driving all the time. She was taken in tow, and arrived in Lowestoft harbour about nine o'clock next morning. There is little doubt the bargemen were right in refusing to abandon the *Decima*, for in spite of being blown on the Scroby in 1938 after her crew had been taken out of her she survived to be still in the Goldsmith fleet when that company celebrated its centenary in 1948.

The *Alfred Corry* and her crew reached home at 1pm after a long and tiring night's work. The crew received £50 as their share of the salvage.

Sam May was at home ill when one Sunday evening, 8th March, 1908, a Belgian ketch, the *Charles Yvonne*, of Ostend, mistook the new Southwold harbour works for Lowestoft, whence she was bound with empty herring barrels. She got on the Hayle Sand, nearly opposite the lifeboat houses, and immediately put out a flare, although the weather was not bad. Several men went off in a punt, laid out an anchor and started to heave her off. Meantime, the captain sent word for the lifeboat and some of the crew came ashore; one refused to go aboard again.

The *Rescue* was launched in charge of the second coxswain, Charles Jarvis, and the vessel was got off and taken to Lowestoft by some of the lifeboatmen, the lifeboat returning ashore. The share of salvage received by the lifeboatmen was only £7, the punt's crew receiving the lion's share. Of course, the Institution in accordance with their rules paid the balance up to the usual scale.

In October, 1908, with the new harbour at Southwold in full swing and the beach very bad for launching, it was decided to remove the *Alfred Corry* to the harbour; a platform was constructed for her near the Ferry, a warp was laid out to sea from the South Pier, and all arrangements were made for working her out of the harbour. Experience showed this

A steam drifter approaching the newly-built herring market in Southwold harbour in November, 1909. In the foreground is the iron paddle tug *Pendennis*.

to be a great improvement; not only could the boat be got off much more quickly and with fewer people but she was launched into smooth water and the crew went off dry and comfortable instead of being drenched in the breakers while launching from the beach. One unforeseen result of the change was that owing to the extra distance to the Ferry the younger men outran the older generation, and young blood formed a much greater proportion of the crew.

The first service from the new harbour occurred on 8th December, 1908, when the spritsail barge *Maria*, of Rochester, got into difficulties while running into the harbour in a moderate SSW gale and let go her anchor between the pierheads. The ebb tide drove her out again and into broken water behind the head of the North Pier, where the anchor held, but the sea was breaking over her.

The *Alfred Corry* was launched about 4pm. She sailed out, took off the two men in a very few minutes, and returned at once to the harbour. Later on, when the tide flowed, the lifeboat went out again with the harbour tug *Pendennis* to endeavour to save the barge, but the lifeboatmen were unable to get on board on account of the sea, which was becoming worse. Eventually the *Maria* drove ashore just north of the lifeboat house, but she was got off and into the harbour next day without great damage.

The spritsail barge *Maria* aground to the north of the lifeboat house after the *Alfred Corry* had taken off the crew of two.

A fleet of between thirty and forty Lowestoft and Kessingland shrimpers was surprised by a sudden severe squall on 2nd August, 1909, the August Bank Holiday. The wind being NE they ran for Southwold harbour, accompanied by the Lowestoft and Pakefield lifeboats; the Kessingland lifeboat was also launched, but returned home. In the opinion of Sam May and other lifeboatmen on the North Pier the Southwold lifeboat was not wanted and could do no good, there being already three afloat; she was not launched, and all those present exerted themselves in assisting the shrimpers into harbour, the boats and the two lifeboats all getting in without difficulty.

Unfortunately the lifeboatmen from Lowestoft and Pakefield told the Southwold men their boat ought to have been off, and chided them for launching only when they liked, and so forth. This soon bred trouble, and when the gun fired for the annual bank holiday parade that afternoon the bulk of the men refused duty.

However, a crew of youngsters was mustered, and they took the boat round the town and launched her as usual, in spite of a nasty sea and the hostile attitude of most of the men. The regrettable but inevitable sequel was the abandonment of the bank holiday parade, which had annually resulted in a substantial collection towards the funds of the Southwold branch.

That was a busy period for the Southwold lifeboat. On 28th October, 1909, Coxswain May launched the *Alfred Corry* into a moderate gale at ENE to go to a steamer showing urgent signals. She proved to be the ss *Hermina*, of Rotterdam, bound to Dieppe with coal, which was in trouble with her steering gear collapsed. The captain engaged the lifeboat to assist him into Harwich, and this was successfully accomplished with the aid of two tugs. Having been launched at 7.45am, the lifeboat got to Harwich at about 6.30pm, and returned home to her station the following day. The salvage claim was settled at £200.

The Aldeburgh lifeboat took the crew out of a spritsail barge near the Sizewell Bank during the early morning of 3rd December, 1909. The lifeboat was damaged and the barge looked like foundering, so the Aldeburgh men left her at daylight and ran to Lowestoft, where the master reported that his vessel had sunk. From Southwold Cliff the barge was kept under close observation, however, and when about 2pm it was learnt that the Aldeburgh men had gone home it was decided to launch the *Alfred Corry*. Sam May took her off to the barge, the *Eureka*, of Harwich, bound to Rochester with oats. Built at Harwich in 1880, the *Eureka* was one of thirteen vessels bearing that name on the British register at the turn of the century. Among them was another spritsail barge named *Eureka*, built at Maldon in 1891 and owned and registered at Colchester.

Just before the Southwold men got to her the *Eureka* was boarded by some Ramsgate smacksmen. The lifeboat took the barge in tow and got her into Southwold harbour just at dark. A salvage action brought by the lifeboatmen and smacksmen jointly was heard at Lowestoft and £200 awarded, but the defendants appealed to the High Court, which ordered a new trial. To save further expense and delay the case was settled for £175. The lifeboatmen's share was doled just over a year afterwards, on 18th December, 1910, and by a remarkable coincidence the *Eureka* sailed into the harbour again the following morning.

The *Alfred Corry* was launched about 3am on 24th January, 1910, to the assistance of the Lowestoft smack *Integrity*, ashore near Covehithe in moderate weather. The lifeboat carried out two anchors, and when a tug arrived the lifeboatmen assisted to get the smack off and into Lowestoft about nine in the morning. The lifeboat's share of salvage was £50.

That month saw the retirement after sixty years' lifeboat service of seventy-eight-year-old Ballintine Brown, who had held the office of leading launcher for sixteen years. The Institution gave him a most welcome gratuity of £5.

Another smack ashore at Covehithe led to the *Alfred Corry* being called out on 28th December, 1910. It was a very dark night as the lifeboat went out, and during the excitement a boy named Stedman fell into the river between the piers. The tide was running out strongly, and Stedman would almost certainly have drowned if a young fisherlad, James Robert Brabben May, had not heard him cry out. May at once jumped in and held him up until a rope was thrown from the pier and they were got out. For his brave action May received the Royal Humane Society's medal and a silver watch from the Carnegie Hero Fund, as well as other rewards. The name of May was again to the fore.

The lifeboatmen found the Lowestoft smack *Excelsior* ashore on the main, so six hands were put on board, an anchor and warp laid out, and the vessel's head hove round. At that stage a tug arrived from Lowestoft with agents of the insurance club to which the smackowner belonged, and they took charge; the lifeboat returned home. The resulting salvage claim was settled for £16.

The winter of 1911-12 was a record one for the Southwold lifeboats, which were off six times on service, saving three crews, one vessel and a boat. The first service on 4th October, 1911, resulted in the *Alfred Corry* saving a fisherman and a visitor from Kessingland who had been after herring in a small boat, and the next effective service came on 22nd December when Sam May took the *Alfred Corry* to a vessel which was firing flares opposite the harbour. Several barges had earlier run into the harbour for shelter from a rising southerly gale, and it was much too bad for any ordinary boat to get out. Rain was being blown before the wind, which was blowing dead into the harbour; the lifeboat had to be tracked down to the pierhead, and just succeeded in getting clear of the South Pier. May and his crew found the vessel to be another barge, the *Beryl*, of Faversham, whose crew were anxious to get into Southwold for shelter.

Second coxswain Charles Jarvis, who was also a harbour pilot, was put aboard with three other men, and they tried to get the vessel into the harbour, but the tide and wind set her into Dunwich Bight close to the shore. At one time it seemed that the barge would be blown ashore, and the lifeboat stood by to take the people out, but the wind eastered a little and she was able to claw off the lee shore, weathering Thorpe Ness about a quarter of a mile. The captain then asked the men to take him to Harwich, and they proceeded through a heavy sea until about 2am, when they sighted the Cork light, the lifeboat running alongside under bare poles.

At this juncture the wind flew off from the NNW, making it quite impossible to get the barge into Harwich, and the captain said they must go to Faversham, where the vessel was bound. Accordingly she was accompanied all the way across the Thames Estuary to Kent by the lifeboat, and anchored there in safety about 4pm next day.

All hands had a good rest that night, and about 2pm the following day they left in a strong wind at south for the homeward journey of about seventy miles. The boat arrived safely in Southwold harbour about two o'clock on Christmas morning, after an absence of fifty-five hours, and the waits came down to the harbour to give the men a Christmas welcome, singing carols as the boat came in.

The committee considered this an unusually good service and specially commended Coxswain May, having regard to the weather, the exceptional difficulties experienced in navigating the vessel to a safe port, the number of hours engaged in actual service, and the length of time the boat was absent on duty. The Institution endorsed this by awarding May a framed certificate of service and a handsome pair of binoculars. A salvage action was brought at the Admiralty Court in London, and £100 was awarded to the lifeboatmen.

Sam May was also in charge during a gallant service on the night of 17th January, 1912, almost the anniversary of the terrible gale of 1881 in which the *Martina Maria* was wrecked opposite Centre Cliff. At the height of a very heavy gale at SE by E information was received from the Coastguard that a schooner was ashore at Misner with the crew in the rigging. The *Alfred Corry* was launched in record time, towed down to the pierhead, and sailed out in a most splendid manner through a very heavy sea. In about an hour she was at the wreck, and the crew let go the anchor to veer down. It was just after dark, and the sea was tremendous.

No sooner did the boat come to her anchor than the cable snapped, and the lifeboat was in the greatest danger of being swept ashore. With incredible smartness the lifeboatmen set sail again, and the boat sailed off to sea and round outside the vessel. The second anchor was let go inside the ship, and the crew of four men and the captain's wife were taken out of the rigging.

With the rescued people safely aboard, the lifeboat sailed back to Southwold, arriving home soon after 7.30pm, having sailed six miles out and six miles back in a very heavy gale, and taken out a crew, in little over three hours. The vessel was the *Voorwaarts*, of Groningen, bound from

The Dutch schooner *Voorwaarts* of Groningen ashore at Minsmere in January 1912. The *Alfred Corry* had taken the crew of four and the captain's wife out of the rigging and landed them in Southwold harbour.

Emden to Southampton with loam.

As she entered the harbour the lifeboat was thrown against the North Pier by a heavy sea, but fortunately without sustaining any very serious damage.

While the *Alfred Corry* was away tremendous excitement was aroused in the town by a large Norwegian barque, the *Idun*, of Christiansand, for Cadiz in ballast, coming ashore exactly opposite the lighthouse. The lifeboat gun was immediately fired, and the *Rescue* was quickly got out and dragged by hand up the hill, through Pinkney's Lane, Trinity Street and North Parade to the Grand Hotel, where she was got over the breakwater and afterwards launched from the carriage near the Steamboat Pier. A heavy sea was breaking on the shoal at the time.

Contrary to orders the men put the boat's mast on shore so that they could row better. When, owing to an error of judgment, they missed the wreck they were unable to fetch her again against tide and sea, and they were obliged to anchor and wait. Had the mast been on board they could have sailed back into position.

Meantime the rocket brigade had fired several rockets over the vessel, which was now within hailing distance, and eventually the whole crew of nine were saved by the apparatus. The lifeboat came ashore at the Gunhill

Crowds watch in the darkness as the lifesaving company fire a line-carrying rocket to the Norwegian barque *Idun*, ashore on Southwold beach.

Above the barque *Idun,* ashore on Southwold beach on 17th January 1912, after her crew had been landed by the rocket lifesaving apparatus team. Two photos by E.R.Cooper. On the left, the crew of the *Idun.*

about 10pm. Early next morning the Ramsgate smack *Olive* was driven ashore within a quarter of a mile of where the *Voorwaarts* lay, but owing to the snowstorm she was not seen. Fortunately the sea washed her up so high that the crew were able to drop off the bowsprit on to the shore, where they were discovered later in the morning.

The *Idun* became a total wreck, her hull being sold for £65 and broken up where it lay. The *Voorwaarts,* an almost new iron schooner, was got off by the lifeboatmen on the Sunday following and, with the assistance of a tug, was got safely into Lowestoft, although her rudder was gone. The salvage agreement was £250, contrasting strongly with the £100 awarded in the case of the *Beryl.* It shows how much worse lifeboatmen were treated for long and arduous services in saving a vessel from going ashore and getting lost or damaged than for getting a vessel off after she had stranded and perhaps suffered much injury; the moral is obvious, but the principle entirely wrong.

Never mind, Sam May had his reward. "Goot man," said the captain's wife, as she patted Sam on his broad back, when they came to tea with us.

In recognition of this most meritorious service the Netherlands

The crew of the *Voorwarts* and the captain's wife, who had been taken for one of the crew by the lifeboatmen at the time of the rescue because she had donned her husband's clothes in an endeavour to keep warm.

Government awarded a silver medal to Coxswain May and bronze medals to the remainder of the crew who risked their lives on that terrible night. These awards were due to be presented on 11th September, 1912, but the ceremony had to be put off for an hour or so; both the coxswain and the secretary were off in the *Rescue* assisting the brigantine *George Casson* into

The Dutch schooner *Voorwarts* is towed off Minsmere beach by the Yarmouth tug *George Jewson*, from which E.R.Cooper took this photograph.

The brigantine *George Casson* of Carnarvon lying in Southwold harbour after being brought in by the Southwold No 2 lifeboat *Rescue* in September 1912.

Southwold harbour, leaky and with a heavy list. Registered at Carnarvon, the *George Casson* was one of that fleet of fine little ships that sailed from Portmadoc with Welsh slates to clothe the roofs of Victorian houses all round Britain.

Then came the 1914-18 war, with its constant worries and anxieties. Most of the best lifeboatmen left for service in various ways, but all the same the lifeboats were afloat sixteen times, saving eighteen lives and six vessels. One of the vessels saved was the ketch barge *Zenobia*, of London, a fine coasting barge built at Ipswich in 1886, which was assisted into Southwold by the *Rescue* on 5th February, 1915, and another was the oil tanker *Batoum*, torpedoed in the Bay on 18th July of the same year. Five of her crew were killed by the explosion, but with the assistance of a tug which I ordered from Lowestoft and the Aldeburgh lifeboat this valuable steamer was safely brought to anchor in Aldeburgh Bay. She was afterwards taken to London and repaired. That was the last time James

The Southwold No 2 lifeboat *Rescue* is launched into a gale, a photograph taken by Mrs. Cooper, her husband is in the boat, standing by the mizzen mast.

Cable and Sam May met on a salvage job.

In November of that same year the *Alfred Corry* got the 299-ton barquentine *John*, of Grimsby, off Sizewell Bank and anchored her in safety. She was on a voyage from Curacao, and the captain had lost himself because all the coastal lights had been extinguished. Later that night the writer went off to her with provisions and a man to act as pilot; he took her to Harwich.

The crew of the *Alfred Corry* had a terrible time at the wreck of the brigantine *Carmenta*, ashore at Sizewell on 23rd February, 1916. Coxswain May had succeeded in bringing the *Alfred Corry* alongside and making a rope fast, but before the crew could do anything a tier of huge seas rolled in over the bank and swept the lifeboat from end to end. Everybody was washed aft, and some went overboard, while the boat lay aground full up with water.

To save themselves and the boat they had to cut the cable and run for Aldeburgh, leaving the crew to be saved by the rocket brigade. It was the only time they ever turned tail, and then only because the lifeboat lay on the ground between the seas and the relieving valves could not clear her quick enough.

Sam May's active service came to an end when on 25th October, 1917,

A wreath is laid from the motor lifeboat *Mary Scott* on 11th November 1927, above the wreck of the ss *Mangara*, sunk in Solebay during the First World War. E.R. Cooper is standing behind the clergyman.

he and his crew assisted the ketches *Fiducia* and *William Grant* into Lowestoft. Like James Cable and countless others, he found the war too much for him. Acting on medical advice, he retired on pension in 1918, to the great regret of the committee and all connected with the lifeboat, some of whom were hard to please.

During part of his time May served a term on Southwold Town Council. He also joined the Volunteers, and was to be seen cheerfully tramping round the drill hall, forming fours and performing feats with a rifle with an earnest energy which perhaps had something to say to his breakdown in health.

Massive and burly, his was an impressive figure. Once, when in London on a salvage case, a taxi was called, and behold Sam could not get through the doorway. They tried him broadside on, but there was very little difference, and a crowd soon collected to see this mighty man of the sea being pushed and pulled through an entrance ample for most cockneys.

"I don't like them taxi things", was his verdict, "you aren't properly in afore they go 'tick', and away go a pint, and you can hardly say knife afore that go 'tack', and there's another pint gone."

The burly figure of Sam May in oilskins and kapok lifejacket.

On an earlier occasion he rode in a horse bus and told us how, "We ha'n't been aboard five minutes afore the port hoss fell down, and there we were in a proper frap."

It was perhaps this ready fund of quaint phrase and his cheery Jack Blunt style that made him so many friends, but there was sterling worth behind. Although of such fine physique his was not a strong constitution, and he suffered much before giving in. Even in retirement his failing heart was in the work, and after that dreadful night of 29th September, 1918, when the *Pomona* was ashore at Sizewell, he said to me next morning, "I heard you keep firing the gun, and I knew you were in trouble, if you'd come for me I should 'a gone, and that would 'a kilt me."

When the end came, on 18th May, 1923, the *East Anglian Daily Times* remarked that May was one of the best-known men of Southwold, immensely popular among visitors and in his native town. By his seat in church is a brass inscribed:

Samuel Charles May, Coxswain of the Lifeboat, Town Councillor, Benefactor of the Church, 1923. In Grateful Remembrance.

From the roof overhead swings a model of the *Alfred Corry*, the pride of his life.

Alongside his great uncle's memorial lies our Storm Warrior, and on his stone are these lines:

His Anchor was the Holy Word,
His Rudder Blooming Hope,
The Love of God His Maintops'l
And Faith His Sailing Rope.

He was a man in a thousand, and he was my friend.

6 Heroes of the Holm

MANY BOLD and daring deeds have been performed in lifeboats on and around the Holm, Newcome and Corton sands, those banks lying a short distance seaward of Lowestoft Ness that protect the anchorage known in years gone by as Corton and Kirkley Roads, or the North and South Roads. In this anchorage many hundreds of ships would seek shelter from every gale in the days of sail, from what old Manship called "the great rage of the sea".

In Suckling's *Suffolk* it is stated that Robert Sparrow, of Worlingham Hall, founded a lifeboat society at Lowestoft on 6th September, 1800, and that a lifeboat was built the next year at a cost of £105. Lowestoft can thus claim one of the first two lifeboats on the Suffolk coast, the other being built at the same time for Woodbridge Haven. Both were built by Henry Greathead, of South Shields, one of those who claim to be the inventor of the lifeboat.

Long before that time there had been wrecks and rescues along this part of the coast. One of the first recorded catastrophes was the great gale of 24th December, 1739, when sixteen ships were ashore between Yarmouth and Lowestoft, and every soul lost. Again, on 15th December, 1759, twenty-two vessels were blown ashore between Yarmouth and Kessingland, and most of them were lost with all hands.

Gillingwater in his *History of Lowestoft* describes another December gale which occurred in 1770, when at least twenty-five ships and 200 men were estimated to have been lost. A pilot boat was launched when the weather moderated, but it was unable to save the few who had survived thus far, although £10 reward was offered, and all perished as the ships broke up.

John Wesley saw the power of the sea when he was in Lowestoft on

79

20th November, 1776. He narrates in his journal how the wind was ready to take him off his feet; a boat was driven from her moorings and like to be swallowed up, whereupon five stout men put off and, rowing for life, saved the three men on board.

The lifeboat that was built for Lowestoft was of what came to be called the North Country type. When it was taken out on trials by twelve men on 2nd March, 1801, it was stated that "in the opinion of the best judges, she is well calculated to answer the purpose intended," but the beachmen never had confidence in her and preferred to use their own yawls.

One must bear in mind the firm belief of the old-time Lowestoft and Yarmouth beachmen that the sands were their private property, and that buoys, beacons, lights and anything tending to reduce casualties were infringements of their rights and were no better than robbery. This feeling might have been in part responsible for the unpopularity of the first lifeboat, but she was evidently a surf boat, for use under oars where a ship was stranded on the main and unsuitable for service on distant sands such as those that lie off our coast.

The *Naval Chronicle* for 1802 tells us that Greathead's standard lifeboat was 30ft by 10ft, rowing ten oars, double banked, steered by an oar, and capable of being rowed either end first. It had a distinctly curved keel and a lining and outside belt of cork, and cost £165.

The *Naval Chronicle* also reports the House of Commons inquiry in 1802 at which Captain Gilfred Lawson Reed, an Elder Brother of Trinity House, stated that he had the management of the Lowestoft lifeboat and had her launched for trial when the sea was very heavy. It took an hour to launch her, and then, owing to one of the plugs having been left out, she filled with water before she reached the sands. She had to return, and was safely beached although full of water. Captain Reed said that the lifeboat had been out only twice, and the men had no experience of her. He admitted, though, that they were unwilling to go off in her, and that she had not at that time been employed on service.

According to the *Ipswich Journal* of 18th February, 1804, the Greathead boat at Bawdsey had just had a successful trial and had saved the crew of a collier brig, the *Pallas*, which had gone ashore and sunk. A long letter in the same paper for 13th October following was addressed to the Lowestoft sailors by the surviving promoter, with respect to the manning of the lifeboat, which had never been used for service. The letter concluded by saying that in the event of failure to make use of her, he would look out for a situation where a more worthy race of men would gladly accept the advantages which they had refused.

Although his name was not given, the surviving promoter was of course Robert Sparrow. His co-promoter, the Reverend Francis Bowness, had died in May, 1801, nine months before the arrival of the boat.

The Lowestoft boat was moved in 1805 to Gorleston, but when HM gun-brig *Snipe* was wrecked there on 18th February, 1807, an occasion when Captain George Manby related that he saw sixty-seven people drowned for want of some means of rescue, nobody seems to have thought of going for the lifeboat.

Robert Sparrow became convinced that nothing could be done with the Greathead boat in the vicinity of Lowestoft, and in 1807 he employed Lionel Lukin, recognised as one of the inventors of early lifeboats, to design a boat for Lowestoft. Lukin, sensible fellow, consulted the local beachmen and obtained their views before designing a lifeboat on the lines of the local beach yawls.

Under Lukin's supervision, Batchelor Barcham built the new lifeboat, the first sailing lifeboat, at Lowestoft in 1807. The boat came under the control of the Suffolk Humane Society, an organisation formed the year before. Lord Rous was president, and the boat was named *Frances Ann* after his eldest daughter, born in 1790.

The *Frances Ann* was 40 feet long, 10 feet 6 inches beam and 3 feet deep, and rowed fourteen oars, though she was primarily a sailing boat rigged, like the beach yawls, with two or three lugsails. To give her buoyancy she was fitted with empty casks under the thwarts and in bow and stern.

The new boat was launched one Thursday in November, 1807, in heavy rain and taken out on trials. The *Ipswich Journal* tells us that "After sailing in various directions, she reached the North-end of Corton Sand, upon which the sea and surf were very high. The utility of the boat was eminently shewn in turning the whole length upon the sand without shipping any water.

"When she came off the sand, the plugs were taken up, and the water suffered to rise as high as the air casks, which were lashed within the boat, would allow. She then stretched under a press of sail to Pakefield; the water with which her bottom was filled, did not appear to retard her progress. There were 16 persons in the boat, including some gentlemen who had volunteered their services. Tho' all of them got over to the leeward side, and some of them stood on the gunwale, yet from all their weight, the press of sail and the plugs still open, her side was not depressed, nor did the water within encrease."

It is sometimes said that Lukin's lifeboat was based on other craft than a beach yawl, but the *Ipswich Journal* recorded specifically that "this boat is built after a model which the Lowestoft seamen consider to be best

The Lowestoft lifeboat *Frances Ann* setting off on 22nd October, 1820, to the Woodbridge sloop *Sarah & Caroline* on the Newcome Sand, from a painting in the Lowestoft and East Suffolk Maritime Museum at Sparrows Nest, Lowestoft. She saved the crew of five from the sloop and also took off seven men from the brig *George* of London, which sank soon afterwards.

adapted to their shore, for rowing, for sailing, for stowage, and for every other useful purpose." Could that be anything other than a beach yawl?

With the new boat in service the old Greathead boat, "found on trial to be unfit for this coast, because of the distance from the sands on which shipwrecks generally happen, and on account of the difficulty of rowing the boat from the shore," was put up for sale.

82

The *Frances Ann* was soon in service, for on 24th February, 1808, she was launched when two colliers ran aground on the sands off Lowestoft. She did not actually rescue anyone, for the Gorleston boats were able to get there first by dint of both wind and tide being against the Lowestoft boat; but the Gorleston men did nothing until the lifeboat was very near, and then, afraid that they might lose their prize, they boarded the vessel to which they had all been heading. Both colliers were eventually got off.

We cannot now tell how busy the *Frances Ann* might have been, but the next service to be recorded came on 14th December, 1809, in a tremendous gale that strewed the beach with wreckage. The collier *Catherine*, of Sunderland, was in trouble on the Holm Sand, and as soon as it was realised that a survivor was still on board the *Frances Ann* was launched. The crew of the lifeboat had a very difficult job in getting him on board; because he was already suffering severely from exposure they decided not to haul him through the water on a rope but instead ran the lifeboat in close to the wreck to snatch him from his precarious perch. It was a risky procedure, and although he was hauled aboard he was crushed between the boat and the wreck in the process, several of his ribs being broken. Some weeks later, however, the *Norwich Mercury* was able to report that after being given "every possible care and attention" the survivor, the carpenter of the *Catherine*, had recovered sufficiently to return home.

The lifeboat committee at Lowestoft seems also to have had one of Manby's line-throwing mortars, and it was used on 13th January, 1810, to rescue seven men from the hoy *Elizabeth Henrietta*, of Papenberg, when she went ashore at Kessingland. The master perhaps remained with his ship too long, for he was lost when she broke up. The mortar was used again on 10th November the same year to save eight men from one of three ships ashore at Corton, but when a vessel struck the sands opposite Lowestoft and the crew were seen clinging in the rigging for a long time nobody was willing to man the lifeboat; the *Suffolk Chronicle* reported that "the best sailors were engaged at Corton." The lifeboat was hauled down to the water's edge, but although twenty-five guineas (£26.25) were offered by some gentlemen the men on the beach refused to go out, alleging not only that the danger was too great but that they had not been rewarded for earlier services.

There seems to have been no permanent coxswain at this time, and the crew was made up of pilots and beachmen. No doubt the senior pilot present took charge when the boat was needed. When the lifeboat was launched on Friday, 13th January, 1815, to a vessel lying among the breakers on the Corton Sand the crew consisted of four pilots, Henry May, David Burwood, James Cullingham junior and Henry Beverley Disney, and fourteen beachmen, Cornelius Ferrett, William Ayers, Samuel and John Spurden, Robert Watson, James Websdale junior, Samuel Butcher junior, Bartholomew Allerton, James Farrer junior, Peter Smith, George Burwood, Matthew Colman, Edward Ellis junior and James Stebbens.

There are names among that crew which are still well remembered in Lowestoft. Henry Beverley Disney, for instance, was a man of thirty-two who had obtained his pilot's licence only five years before; he renewed it for the last time in 1870 when he was eighty-seven, and by then he had gained a considerable reputation as a lifesaver.

"The alacrity with which these brave fellows leaped on board the life

The beach yawl *Happy New Year* under sail in Lowestoft harbour.

boat is scarcely to be described," wrote the Reverend Bartholomew Ritson, curate of Lowestoft and secretary of the Suffolk Humane Society.

Three of the pilot yawls had already put off, but it was found that because of the tremendous sea on the sand it was quite impossible for the yawls to get near the wreck without the greatest danger. The men in the yawls thereupon signalled to the pilot lookout, at the top of High Street not far from the lighthouse, that there were three men on the wreck, the sloop *Jeanie* of Hull, and the *Frances Ann* was launched to the rescue.

"After encountering much difficulty and danger in passing the breakers they came near to the vessel in sight of hundreds of spectators, who from the heights were beholding with astonishment their admirable nautical skill and dauntless courage, at the same time trembling between hope and fear for their safety," wrote Mr. Ritson. "Heaven in its mercy smiled propitious on their endeavours, and rewarded the exertions of these brave men with success, and they had the heartfelt joy of bringing the three shipwrecked mariners to shore without any accident."

We might smile today at Mr. Ritson's rather pious way of expressing himself, but there is no doubt that he had a good understanding of the problems the men faced out at sea. He went on to tell how the little *Jeanie* had left Hull with a cargo of potatoes for London on the Thursday morning, and about midnight when off the Haisborough Gat sprang a leak. The water gained so fast that the crew had to run her on the sand to prevent her foundering.

Members of the Suffolk Humane Society were delighted with this success and immediately voted five guineas (£5.25) to the eighteen men who made up the lifeboat crew. "In the case above stated," Mr. Ritson went on, "a most favourable opportunity has been afforded to the Suffolk Humane Society of proving to the public the comparative safety and consequent utility of the Lowestoft Life Boat, that with it has been happily effected, as far as human means can avail, that which could not have been effected by any other boat from this beach; and what is most desirable, all doubts respecting its eligibility as a sea boat, have now been cleared up, and all former prejudices to its disadvantage, which have long been known to have existed in the minds of our seamen, removed. . .".

In spite of Mr Ritson's triumphant words, the Lowestoft men still distrusted the lifeboat, and perhaps they distrusted even more the gentlemen who made up the membership of the Suffolk Humane Society.

After all, which one of those men was capable of taking the boat off to a wreck?

During a December storm in 1819 a brig grounded near the shore "and laid in such a position as none, after several efforts, could relieve the crew, eight in number. They clung to the wreck, and their cries during the evening were distinctly heard in the streets. They all perished within a few yards as it were of almost the whole population of Lowestoft."

If there was work to be done, it was to their yawls and gigs that the beachmen ran, not to the lifeboat. It required a strong man to show that the lifeboat did indeed have a place on Lowestoft beach.

Lieutenant Samuel Thomas Carter, a member of an old-established Suffolk family from the Sudbury area, settled in Lowestoft after being retired from the Royal Navy on half pay in 1813, along with many more naval officers who were no longer required as the Napoleonic Wars neared their end. And it was perhaps natural that he should take an interest in the lifeboat.

Carter had joined the Navy as a first-class volunteer in 1800 and had attained the rating of midshipman later that year. His apprenticeship to the sea was a long one, and it was not until 1808 that he was confirmed in the rank of lieutenant, a rank he was to hold for nearly forty years before being promoted to commander, retired.

We know little of Lieutenant Carter's personal life, except that the year after finding himself "on the beach" he married his cousin, the daughter of a rector of Margate, and together they brought up a family in their home in London Road, Lowestoft. What we do know is that he was a superb leader and a fine seaman, and that in the course of a most distinguished career in the *Frances Ann* he helped to save a good many lives.

We do not even know when he first went in the lifeboat, but he was in charge when the *Frances Ann* was launched on 22nd October, 1820, into a heavy SSW gale which increased in the course of that Sunday morning into almost a hurricane. About midday a vessel seeking shelter in the Roads struck on the sand as she came through the Stanford Channel and went to pieces within minutes. All the crew were lost, as was the crew of another ship which also hit the sand. A third vessel, the little sloop *Sarah and Caroline*, of Woodbridge, was luckier when she struck the Newcome. The mast remained standing as she filled and sank, and the crew of five took refuge in the rigging.

Because of the ebb tide and the wind it was impossible for a boat from Lowestoft beach to reach the Newcome. The *Frances Ann* was launched and towed a considerable distance along the beach to the southward so that she could sail out to the wreck, but the tow was let go too soon and the boat fell to leeward of her. It was not until the tide began to flow that the lifeboat was able to reach the *Sarah and Caroline* and to pick up the five men just in the nick of time; one poor fellow was so far gone that he was about to drop from his hold in the rigging.

As they were trying to reach the wreck the lifeboatmen were hailed by a collier brig, the *George*, of London. Having got the men out of the rigging the lifeboatmen turned to the collier, which they found was in a sinking state. They took the crew of seven out of her, and landed all twelve safely on Lowestoft beach; the survivors from the *Sarah and Caroline* were suffering so severely from exposure and exhaustion that they could hardly walk.

Bartholomew Ritson could now answer the critics who had been throwing doubt not only on the effectiveness of the lifeboat but on the efforts of the Suffolk Humane Society. Referring to the fact that "those who had the care and conduct of the lifeboat were most unjustly and petulantly assailed by an anonymous writer," Mr. Ritson said that the rescue had "most forcibly demonstrated the utility of the lifeboats in general. . .and that of Lowestoft in particular." He might have added that they now had a man in charge who was going to ensure that the boat was used as effectively as human endeavour would allow.

Nonetheless, Lieutenant Carter was still up against the intransigence of beachmen who regarded the coast as their preserve and resented anything that they felt infringed their rights. On 7th December, 1821, during a SSE gale the brig *Westmoreland*, bound from Stockton-on-Tees for London with a general cargo, unshipped her rudder and was driven on the Newcome Sand. When she hoisted a signal of distress five boats, including the lifeboat, put off from Lowestoft beach to her assistance.

It seems that the yawl *Seaman's Assistance*, belonging to Denny's Company, was the first to run up alongside the brig, and therefore in the beachmen's code Denny's Company "had the job". The crew of the brig threw a line to the beachmen, who hauled the yawl alongside the weather bow, and two of the beachmen, John Stebbings and William Butcher, boarded the brig.

There are conflicting accounts of what happened next. It seems that the *Frances Ann* was brought alongside the brig and made fast by a line, but that the line was cut by somebody, said to be one of the beachmen. It was given later in evidence at the Admiralty Court that when Lieutenant Carter's second-in-command, a young naval officer named Samuel Fielding Harmer, made the lifeboat's line fast he was greeted by a chorus of disapproval from the beachmen still in the yawl, who shouted "Cut her away!"

As the tide rose the brig floated off the sand, but it was then found she was taking water very badly, so she was run ashore on the flats off Pakefield after a young woman and a boy had been taken off by the yawl. Lieutenant Carter, seeing the *Seaman's Assistance* leaving the wreck, assumed that the yawl had taken off the entire crew, so the lifeboat left the scene.

In fact Captain Ryder and the crew of the brig had refused to leave. Their predicament was serious, for the wreck was beginning to go to pieces, and by the time the situation became clear darkness had fallen. Although the lifeboat returned to the vicinity of the wreck and stood by for some six hours the crew could not make contact with the men on the *Westmoreland*. Eventually, about 1am, Lieutenant Harmer joined men of Denny's Company in going off in a gig they had hauled from Lowestoft by a team of horses, and leapt from the gig into the rigging; he found only two men still alive in one of the tops.

Fourteen beachmen were later accused of conspiring to prevent assistance being given to a vessel in distress and obstructing the crew of the *Westmoreland* in their endeavour to escape from the vessel, by cutting the rope by which the lifeboat had been made fast, as a consequence of which four men were lost. The beachmen were acquitted of the conspiracy charge, but young William Butcher, who was said to have been responsible for cutting the lifeboat adrift, was bound over on that particular charge.

When Lieutenant Harmer told the court he had seen one of the beachmen cut the rope by which the lifeboat was made fast and had heard him say "Damn your eyes, let go and take that thing ashore, you've no business here!" he was commended by the judge, Lord Stowell, for his actions that day.

"Mr. Harmer, the conduct of you and your brother officers has been highly meritorious," Lord Stowell observed. "And the Grand Jury have recommended that it should be brought before the Admiralty—I shall take care that that is done."

Bartholomew Ritson appeared in court to tell how he had remonstrated with John Denny on the impropriety of cutting away the lifeboat; no doubt he had given him a thorough tongue-lashing. Denny had been unmoved; he had replied that he had done nothing contrary to the usage and custom of boats going out to ships in such situations.

And pilot Henry May, who was one of the lifeboat crew on that occasion, told the court that there was an impression among the beachmen that in cases of ships in distress the doctrine of first come, first served was held with respect to salvage. "If any such impression exists, nothing can be more erroneous," Lord Stowell said. "It is without the slightest foundation of fact. If this case had come before the Court of Admiralty as a question of salvage, I would not have adjudged a single farthing."

His words made no impression on the beachmen, who continued to stick to their own arbitrary rules and customs, and to their own interpretation of the *Westmoreland* case. Folk-memory in Lowestoft retained an entirely different story of a rascally captain who refused to allow his crew to leave the ship and threatened the beachmen with a pistol when they offered to take the crew off.

Within a year some of the beachmen who had figured in the case were dead. In January, 1823, the *Seaman's Assistance* was reported lost with William Butcher, his son William, and six other beachmen. All that was found was an oar, a chest and other gear identified as belonging to the yawl, washed up near Aldeburgh.

The next rescue it has been possible to trace took place on 18th January, 1825, when two brigs struck on the Newcome Sand and a sloop went on the Holm in a strong southerly gale. The lifeboat under Lieutenants Carter and Harmer was launched to the brig *Ann* of Shields, but it was not to be a straightforward rescue. As one newspaper reported:

> The ebb tide was now running strong, and with the assistance of eight horses the boat was towed through a tremendous surf, over Pakefield flats, but the tow rope breaking, they were not able to fetch the vessel but were obliged, after crossing the Newcome, to let go their anchor and wait for the flood tide, so that it was 3.30pm before they were able to beat to windward.

The lifeboatmen had to leave it to the yawl *Trinity*, belonging to Lincoln's Company, to take off the crew of the *Ann*, eight men and two

Beach company lookouts on Lowestoft beach about 1830. At that time boat-building was carried out on the beach.

boys. They had to turn their attention to the sloop *Dorset*, of Ramsgate, which was lying on her beam ends on the Holm with the crew of seven clinging precariously to the masthead.

After repeated attempts Lieutenant Harmer managed to throw a grappling hook into the rigging and the lifeboat was hauled under the masthead. The master dropped into Harmer's arms, and then a few minutes later one of the crew dropped into the lifeboat. But the lifeboatmen were themselves in trouble, with tremendous seas breaking across the wreck and into the lifeboat.

Lieutenant Carter, pilot David Burwood and another lifeboatman were all washed overboard, but their companions hauled them safely back on board. The boat was full of water, and becoming unmanageable.

"For God's sake cut the cable, we shall all be lost!" somebody cried out. There was nothing the lifeboatmen could do to save the other five men on the sloop, the cable had to be cut and the unmanageable lifeboat was washed away from the wreck. The foresail was hoisted just enough to bring the boat round, and the lifeboatmen struggled to regain control.

When, after crossing the Newcome in safety, they reached the beach between seven and eight o'clock that evening the lifeboatmen were so exhausted they had to be helped home by their friends; some had to be carried.

The crew of the second brig, the *Harriett and John*, of Sunderland, had saved themselves by taking to their own boat. The Suffolk Humane Society awarded medals to two pilots who were in the lifeboat as well as to George Yallop, "steersman of the life-boat", and also to the steersman of the *Trinity*, for their work that day.

Just what had gone wrong? It seems that the heavy seas had swamped the lifeboat, which had "reached the shore full of water." At the anniversary meeting of the Suffolk Humane Society the following August "many useful experiments were put into practice under the particular direction of Lieutenant Harmer, by whom a considerable improvement respecting an increase in buoyancy in the lifeboat was proposed, and its utility clearly demonstrated; in consequence of which the plan was adopted, and the necessary alterations will be immediately resorted to."

Did Harmer propose increasing the number of casks lashed within the boat to give buoyancy, or did he even suggest replacing them with shaped airboxes in the style of later lifeboats? And did he propose cutting substantial holes in the bottom of the boat which would be closed with large plugs on handles such as were employed in later boats of the Norfolk and Suffolk type, so that the boat would be flooded when afloat, and any water coming into the boat would find its way out through the plugholes while the boat floated on its aircases? Was he, in fact, the originator of that peculiar system of loose water ballast that pertained in the Norfolk and Suffolk type for more than half a century thereafter?

Alas, we cannot be certain of the answer to those questions, but it does seem that Harmer certainly played a very significant part in lifeboat development, something for which he has never been given credit.

Later that same year the lifeboat was launched to the aid of the brig *Rochester*, of North Shields, which was discovered at daybreak on 20th October aground on the Corton Sand. It was thought that with the ebb tide she could sail to the position of the wreck, but the wind shifted from east of north to NNW, with very heavy squalls, and this proved impossible. The lifeboat was then towed by eight horses down to Corton Rails, from which she could sail off to windward of the wreck, but by then the masts of

91

the brig had gone overboard and the crew had been washed away.

As always happens in such cases there were loud condemnations of the lifeboatmen, answered with some authority by Edmund Norton, a local lawyer who had taken over from Bartholomew Ritson as secretary of the Suffolk Humane Society. "Although the exertions of those on board the lifeboat were not crowned with success, they have the satisfaction of knowing that they used every exertion in their power, and to the best of their judgment," he said in a letter to the *Ipswich Journal*.

Lieutenant Carter and his men had better luck on 17th May, 1828, when they went out to the collier brig *Fawn*, of Sunderland, which had gone on the Corton Sand. The lifeboat picked up the crew, who had left the vessel in their own boat and had by good fortune come safely through the broken water on the sand.

Then in November, 1829, the lifeboatmen had an unusually busy period in a ENE gale which caused numerous casualties up and down the East Anglian coast. On the 23rd Carter and Harmer with a crew of seventeen took the *Frances Ann* to the brig *Thomas and Mary*, of Newcastle, which had run on the Newcome as she came through the Stanford Channel. Lieutenant Carter anchored to windward of the vessel and veered out the cable until the lifeboat was alongside the wreck.

Although the sea broke over the wreck and into the lifeboat the master of the collier, eight men and a boy were successfully taken off and brought safely ashore. The very next day two brigs riding to their anchors off Pakefield were seen to be flying distress signals. As the lifeboat was being got ready one of the brigs slipped her cable and ran for the beach. The *Frances Ann* saved the master and eight men from the other brig, the *Ann* of London, which later went on the beach and broke up.

The two lieutenants were given the thanks of the Suffolk Humane Society, which gave the crews £5 in each instance.

The same afternoon the crew of the *Ranger*, of Whitby, in trouble off Pakefield, was rescued by Henry May and Henry Colby in a punt, and in the evening the beachmen, by means of a rope, saved a man from the *Liverpool Packet*, of Whitehaven; another three men were saved from the maintop of the same vessel about midnight.

That was the end of Lieutenant Harmer's service in the Lowestoft lifeboat, for the following June he was appointed Chief Officer of Coastguard in his native Yarmouth. From then on he was to be found not in the *Frances Ann* but in the Yarmouth lifeboat. In 1831 both Harmer and Carter were presented with silver snuff boxes by the Suffolk Humane Society in recognition of their outstanding work in the lifeboat. Harmer was promoted to commander in 1837, and in the same year was appointed Inspecting Officer of Coastguard at Yarmouth. When his term as Inspecting Officer came to an end he was given command of HMS *Driver*, a steam vessel which was due to be sent out to the China station. News of his death on the China coast in 1843 was received with great sadness at Yarmouth, where "the gallant captain had particularly endeared himself to the seamen of this port by his intrepid bravery on board the life-boat". He was surely no less mourned at Lowestoft.

Lieutenant Carter was therefore in sole charge when he took the *Frances Ann* out to the brig *Clifton* which had gone on the east side of the Corton Sand on 26th November, 1830. The lifeboat rescued the crew of nine and a passenger from the brig, which had been on a voyage from Hamburg to London.

An account of the service in the *Suffolk Chronicle* contained the remark that "scarcely a winter has passed but he has been engaged in these praiseworthy attempts to rescue from destruction his fellow creatures. . . . he has been instrumental in saving the lives of 50 persons. . ."

Lieutentant Samuel Fielding Harmer, RN, who with Lieutentant Carter did such good work in the *Frances Ann*.

Some of the Pakefield beachmen probably owed their lives to Lieutenant Carter and the lifeboatmen when their yawl got into difficulties as they took out the crew of the schooner *Sarah*, of Brixham, on 21st July, 1831. The schooner, laden with coal, had gone aground during a hard southerly "blow." The *Norfolk Chronicle* reported that "but for assistance rendered them by the lifeboat [they] would in all probability have been swamped." The Suffolk Humane Society voted £5 to the lifeboat crew and £7 to the crew of the yawl.

The following March the lifeboat was launched when the timber-laden barge *Richard*, of London, shipped a sea as she came over the Barnard Sand and her stack of timber shifted to leeward. Another sea carried away the tiller and she broached to and upset. The master and the crew of two were got off by the beachmen when the wreck drifted ashore near Lowestoft Ness, but one of the men was already dead.

It was not until January, 1835, that Carter and the *Frances Ann* found themselves in the newspapers again. On Sunday, 18th January, the schooner *Bishop Blaize* struck on the Newcome while on her way from Hull to London with general cargo, and a Pakefield boat which went off to her assistance picked up four of the crew who had left in the ship's boat. It became known on the boat's return that the master, Robert Hunter, and the mate, his son, were still on board the schooner.

"Lieutenant S.T. Carter, RN, with that alacrity which that officer has always shown in many preceding cases, and accompanied with a brave crew (being assisted off by a great many of the inhabitants, the sea making very heavy at the time) proceeded to the vessel, and after many attempts by rowing and sailing, succeeded in rescuing the two poor fellows from their perilous position and landed them safely about 10.30 at night," says the *Norfolk Chronicle*.

A year later, on 4th February, 1836, Lieutenant Carter again had the help of many townspeople in launching the lifeboat when a gale from ENE forced a number of vessels ashore. One of two brigs which had been seen on the Barnard Sand broke up with the loss of all hands, but the lifeboatmen arrived in time to save the only survivor of the other brig, the *Speedwell*, of South Shields. They landed him at Kessingland, and the lifeboat was then towed about three-quarters of a mile to the northward to go to the aid of a third brig, the *David Ricardo*, of London, which was lying on the outer flat.

Most unfortunately Lieutenant Carter was somehow badly injured in the right arm during this operation, and he could not go off in the boat when it was taken out by a mixed crew of Lowestoft and Pakefield men, who were successful in saving the whole crew of seven.

His injury must have healed successfully, for Carter continued to have charge of the lifeboat, and it was to him that a messenger hurried in the evening darkness of 1st November, 1837, to say that a brig had grounded on the south-western end of the Newcome Sand and was showing signals for assistance. Helped by Edmund Norton and many townspeople, Carter launched the *Frances Ann* and after three attempts succeeded in taking off the ten-man crew and four passengers, two men and two women, from the Newcastle trader *Bywell*, which had grounded while on her voyage to the north. A new vessel of 250 tons burthen, the *Bywell* had a cargo of tea and tobacco said to be valued at over £30,000, an enormous sum for those days; unfortunately for the owners it was uninsured. Within a quarter of an hour of the crew and passengers being taken off the *Bywell* fell over on her beam ends and began breaking up, and before long her valuable cargo was floating about in the sea.

Lloyd's awarded Lieutenant Carter a medal "as a mark of the sense entertained by them of his meritorious and humane conduct in saving the crew and passengers of the Newcastle trader." Lieutenant Carter himself gave great credit to Henry Beverley Disney, who seems to have become second-in-command, or second coxswain as we would say today, when Lieutenant Harmer went to Yarmouth, and to the boat's crew for their work that day.

Little more than two months went by before the next service in which he was to be involved. On 10th January, 1838, the *Frances Ann* was launched to the Leith smack *Sir Walter Scott*, which was seen lying at anchor close to the Barnard Sand with a signal of distress flying. It was found she had lost her rudder and was making a great deal of water, but the captain and crew were not disposed to leave her.

The lifeboat took off a woman and a boy and landed them at Benacre. Lieutenant Carter left the lifeboat there, as the captain of the smack had said he might need assistance later; there is no evidence that the lifeboat was required, however.

In 1840 the decision was made to build a larger lifeboat on similar lines to the *Frances Ann* that would be stationed at Pakefield, a few miles south

95

of Lowestoft. The new boat was built by William Teasdel at Yarmouth at a cost of £300 and was 45 feet long by 11 feet beam. On 26th January, 1842, the new Pakefield boat and the *Frances Ann* were jointly involved in rescuing the crew of the collier brig *Thomas Oliver*, which had gone on the Inner Newcome, otherwise known as the Bath House Sand.

The wind was blowing what an eyewitness described as a hurricane and the seas were running "mountains high" when the *Frances Ann* was launched with a crew of twenty-one, including Carter and Disney. The seas broke over the lifeboat, constantly filling her with water, and at one stage Disney was washed overboard; he managed to retain his grasp of a safety line and was hauled back into the boat by his colleagues.

Seven of the eight men on board the *Thomas Oliver* had been hauled through the surf into the lifeboat when the boat's anchor came home. It was only with the greatest difficulty that the damaged lifeboat was manoeuvred under the bowsprit of the brig, the cable was cut and the boat made for the shore with the seven rescued men on board. The eighth man was saved by the Pakefield boat, "manned by a crew endowed with the same high courage and good seamanship which had characterised their neighbours."

Lieutenant Carter was a man of fifty-seven at this time, and the exertions of that day proved almost too much for him. When the boat was beached he was exhausted and had to be carried to a nearby house, "where the usual means having been resorted to, he was after a few hours so far restored as to be able to return to his residence in a chaise."

That was probably Carter's last service. His promotion to commander, retired, in 1844 might have been recognition of his outstanding lifesaving work; more than likely it was merely a matter of seniority.

Somewhat curiously, no further lifeboat services were recorded in the newspapers for some years, except for a brief note that on 17th May, 1843, the *Farnacres*, of and from Sunderland for London with coal, was wrecked on Corton Sand, "crew saved by life-boat".

What we do know is that the *Frances Ann*, known among the beachmen as "the Ol' Mawther," continued to serve at Lowestoft until in 1849 she capsized during one of the tests for lifeboats at the Lowestoft Roads Regatta. It would appear that some of the air casks that were supposed to give her buoyancy were no longer airtight and watertight, and doubtless she was worn out after forty-two years of strenuous service.

In 1850 a new boat was built by Lowestoft boatbuilder Samuel Sparham at a cost of some £200. Yet the *Frances Ann* lived on; to save money the impecunious Suffolk Humane Society transferred her masts and sails to the new boat.

Commander Carter did not long survive his old boat. He died at Stanway, near Colchester, in 1851, having been credited with saving 124 lives during his years as "commander of the life-boat." A fine record.

* * *

We do not know who took over command of the Lowestoft lifeboat from Samuel Carter any more than we know about the later years of the *Frances Ann*. What we do know is that in 1853 Robert Hook was appointed coxswain of the *Victoria*, as the new lifeboat had been named at the Suffolk Humane Society anniversary meeting in August, 1850.

Robert William Hook had been born in Lowestoft in 1828, most likely in or near the aptly-named Mariners Street, close to the North Beach and within sound of the "northering swipe" through which he so often launched in after years. Those were the days when the beach was a hive of industry and the roads inside the sands were crowded with coasters, before the harbour was made at Lowestoft.

On that exposed Ness Hook spent most of his days at fishing, salvage and lifeboat work. Without doubt it was a hard life, but it always made hardy men of whom it had been written centuries before:

Wet and cold cannot make them shrink nor strain
Whom the North Sea hath dyed in grain.

Six feet three in height and with the frame of a Hercules, Hook was well fitted to contend with wind and wave, and when only sixteen he was playing his part in the saving of life and the salving of vessels in trouble on the sands.

One of Hook's earliest adventures was on 21st December, 1847, when he went afloat in the Old Company's yawl *Princess Royal* to the assistance of a vessel driving over the Holm Sand in a heavy easterly gale. On returning from that job they fell in with a Dutch galliot sunk on the Holm, so, lowering sail under the lee, they pulled through the surf right on top of the sand and got off the whole crew. Only three nights later they took six

97

Robert Hook was appointed coxswain of the Lowestoft lifeboat *Victoria* in 1853, at the age of twenty-five. A wonderful portrait by H. Jenkins of Lowestoft.

men out of the brig *Heart of Oak*, aground on the Newcome, full of water. And a bitter cold, blowing Christmas Eve it was too, according to Bob Hook.

The *Victoria* was first launched with Hook in charge on 25th April, 1853, when she took the crew of ten out of the snow *Mary Young*, of Shields, in the Mediterranean trade, which had struck on the Newcome and lost her rudder during a gale of wind. I imagine she was got off later, as she was still in the register in 1866. It is recorded that thirteen vessels in the Roads had flags in their rigging that very dirty day.

The Lowestoft and Pakefield lifeboats became connected with the Royal National Lifeboat Institution in 1855, an arrangement being made by which the Suffolk Humane Society continued to provide the boats while the RNLI took responsibility for rewarding the crews.

In November, 1855, the *Victoria* went out to the brig *Louisa*, of Newhaven, which had gone on the Holm Sand. While standing by the grounded brig the lifeboat herself grounded on the sand, and as the tide dropped she was swept by the waves. Later, though, she was left high and dry and the crew were able to walk across to the *Louisa*. When, many hours later, the rising tide refloated the *Victoria* she took the *Louisa*'s crew of nine ashore.

When the Tuscan barque *Zemira* went on the Newcome in October, 1858, it was not the *Victoria* which went to her aid but the Pakefield lifeboat, a then unnamed boat built by Teasdel at Yarmouth in 1840. The barque very soon began to go to pieces as the seas battered her on the hard sand. First the mainmast went overboard, taking with it four of the thirteen hands, then the mizzen topmast went. The foremast too went overboard as the lifeboat struggled to reach the wreck, and those who could grasped spars and other pieces of wreckage on which they drifted down the Roads.

The Pakefield men found the conditions almost too much for them, and one lifeboatman advised Coxswain Nathaniel Colby to give up as the boat was hit by one sea after another, submerging the men and threatening at every instant to wash them overboard. Coxswain Colby was forced at one stage to throw his arms around a thwart to avoid being washed out of the boat.

"My life's as sweet to me as yours; go we must," he told the man who wanted to give up. They picked up one man after another from drifting pieces of wreckage, the eighth and last survivor being a full two miles from the vessel on the sand. At least one of the rescued Italians was almost naked, for they had thrown off their clothes to be able to swim the better, and the Pakefield men pulled off their own clothes to wrap round them.

It was many years before this rescue, which created a considerable

99

impression both on the local people and on visitors, was forgotten. The wreck of the *Zemira* proved a hazard to shipping for some years, and the brigantine *Courier*, of Arbroath, sank after striking it when standing on for Pakefield Gat.

Hook's great year appears to have been 1859, when the autumn gales were unusually severe and the services of the Lowestoft lifeboat more fully recorded than they had been in earlier years. On 26th October during a regular southerly buster the schooner *Lord Douglas*, of Dundee, which was riding in the North Roads, parted from her anchors and foundered off Corton, the crew taking to the rigging. The lifeboat went to her and Hook anchored to windward so that the lifeboat wore down until the crew could heave a line into the schooner's foretop, by means of which five men were dragged through the water into the lifeboat.

The *Victoria's* sails, perhaps those inherited from the *Frances Ann*, were by this time in a very poor state, and the foresail blew out. The crew beached her somewhere between Corton and Lowestoft and tramped home.

That same afternoon the Glasgow schooner *Silva* drove out of the Roads, although she had three anchors down, and she went on the Corton Sand. Hook immediately borrowed another foresail and set off again to the rescue, while the Pakefield men launched their lifeboat and set off. "It was an exciting scene to see her [the *Victoria*] beating up, and a cheering sight to see the gallant Pakefield men with their boat running down to the same spot," wrote a reporter who saw the rescue from the shore. "By some means the Pakefield boat overshot the mark, but the Lowestoft boat was more successful and, having come to windward bore down, and although tremendous breakers at times covered her, rescued the crew."

Yet another schooner was seen in trouble outside the sands. As the *Victoria* set off to help this vessel her borrowed foresail split, so she had to run to leeward and landed the rescued men at Yarmouth. The Pakefield lifeboat went off to the third schooner and towed her to safety.

That was the gale in which the steamer *Royal Charter* was wrecked on the coast of Anglesey with heavy loss of life; it was known for years afterwards as the Royal Charter Gale. Owing to the weather the *Victoria* had to be left at Yarmouth for a couple of days, and she arrived home only just in time to carry out Hook's most distinguished rescue.

It was during the morning of 1st November that beachmen on the South Pier saw the steamer *Shamrock*, of Dublin, heading for the Holm. She struck the sand, as they knew she must, and a signal of distress was hoisted as the beachmen ran to the lifeboat, which was launched off the beach by about a hundred men. Hook and his crew sailed off to the vessel and anchored as close

The *Victoria* under Bob Hook rescuing the crew of fourteen from the Dublin steamer *Shamrock* on 1st November, 1859. It is said that every window along the Lowestoft sea front was occupied by people watching the rescue.

as was safe in a sea which was going over the steamer's mastheads and filling the boat "full and full," as the saying goes.

"We'll be with ye direc'ly, my lads!" roared Bob Hook at the steamer's crew, who were urging the lifeboatmen on. "Only be ready to catch the rope."

As the crew wore the lifeboat down to the ship one of the lifeboatmen took his chance and threw a line to the men on the foc'stle head, and one by one the crew of fourteen were with much difficulty drawn on board the lifeboat, which all the time was lying broadside to the sea and only just clear of the broken water.

Every window along the sea front is said to have been occupied by spectators, who applauded as they saw the last of the fourteen men, the captain, dragged into the lifeboat. The Institution awarded double pay of £1 each and, in testimony of admiration for this and previous distinguished services, awarded its silver medal not only to Coxswain Hook but to Francis Smith, Richard Butcher, Alfred Mewse, Thomas Liffen, James Butcher and William Rose.

There is not space to tell of every one of Bob Hook's rescues, but one should tell of the rescue of eight Austrians from the brig *Osip*, on the Holm again. A Dr. Worthington, perhaps Dr. Frank Worthington who began life as a sailor on board the Yarmouth brig *Elizabeth*, of which my grandfather was part-owner, has left a graphic account of this epic rescue.

Early in the morning of January 13th [1866] a vessel drove on the far end of the Holm Sand and lay exposed to the violence of a severe gale from the south-west with heavy seas. Twelve men were seen on board. The lifeboat put out and battled her way out, but was unable to get near, owing to the heavy masts and spars floating by the side of the wreck. The lifeboat was compelled to cut her cable and leave the wreck. On her return to harbour she took on a new anchor cable. She was then towed out again by the *Rainbow* [Dr Worthington was on board this vessel, an iron paddle tug owned by the Great Eastern Railway]. The atmosphere was thick from fog and rain and the gale still continued. When the lifeboat got back to the wreck they found nothing but the bare stern of the vessel, the remainder being buried in the sands and the breakers, apparently without a human creature upon it. The tug continued to tow as fast as possible and men were seen in the shelter. The lifeboat approached the wreck just as some of the crew were washed off in the direction of the lifeboat. Altogether eight men were rescued out of twelve.

It seems from an Institution report that the captain of the Austrian brig refused the services both of the lifeboat and of a yawl which had put out earlier. Perhaps that is why the lifeboat returned ashore the first time, only putting out a second time when it was obvious the vessel was going to pieces. According to the Institution report the whole crew of twelve was saved.

Then there was the saving of the crew of the brig *William* by the yawl *Happy New Year*. That was the time the yawl grounded on the Holm at low water, some distance from the ship. Hook got into communication with the shipwrecked crew by wading and swimming through the surf in the black dark, whereby all hands were eventually saved, though the ship broke up. Knowing the swipe and power of the surf on the sands, I can hardly find words to express my admiration of this feat of bravery and strength; facing imminent death, alone in the blackness of a stormy night on that treacherous Holm. No wonder the *William's* people were scared when they first heard a lusty hail coming from the midst of that welter of foaming, breaking surges.

Bob Hook was awarded the second service clasp to his silver medal on 1st May, 1873, "in testimony of his general brave services in saving life from shipwreck, and particularly the crew of ten men from the wrecked brig *Expedite*, of Drobak, on November 13, 1872."

By that time the Victoria had been renamed *Laetitia*. She continued to serve, with Hook as coxswain, until replaced in 1876 by a new boat, the *Samuel Plimsoll*, built by the same Samuel Sparham who had built the *Victoria*.

We cannot all expect to be heroes all the time, and many, like Humpty Dumpty, come a purler sooner or later. At Lowestoft the fall from grace came on 28th October, 1882, a day still known by the old hands as "Black Saturday"— whereby hangs a tale of muddle, discontent, and callous indifference to duty which cannot well be passed over without mention.

On Friday, 27th October, a breeze set in, and by midday Saturday it had worked up to a howling gale, with a raging tide and tremendous swell. That afternoon many ships in the Roads were flying distress flags, but nothing was done and the men declined to launch the lifeboat, or even to open the doors of the house, on account of a grievance as to payment for some recent launches. "Let them as rob the crew save the lives" was the reply to protests.

By the evening twenty vessels were ashore between Yarmouth and Southwold with the crews in the rigging, and some lives had already been lost. A couple of visitors were so distressed and enraged at the scene that they went to Bob Hook and called upon him to unlock the doors so that the lifeboat could be got out, and when he demurred they threatened to smash the doors open and show him up in every paper in England.

To be fair, Hook and the beachmen had been busy all day, and when the two visitors banged on his door Hook had just arrived home to change his sodden clothes. The beachmen, who considered themselves no longer to be members of the lifeboat crew after a disagreement earlier in the year, had been active in assisting vessels which ran for the harbour, helping them through the pierheads and mooring them; they had also been helping to get people off the ships that went aground on the beach when they missed the entrance.

The Coastguard had already used the rocket apparatus to save the crew of the collier *Messenger*, of Blyth, together with a number of beachmen who had been attempting to get her off the beach to the south of the harbour, when soon after six in the evening three collier brigs were driven ashore as they tried to enter harbour. The *Susanna Dixon*, of Whitby, and the *Mornington*, of Colchester, were cast ashore about two hours after low water. Then the *Isis*, of Cowes, became unmanageable and drifted into the

Susanna Dixon, whose crew boarded the *Isis* as their own vessel began to break up.

That was when everyone began asking about the lifeboat. The Coastguard with their rocket cart had gone off to Pakefield to save the crew of the brigantine *William Thrift*, and it was soon realised that only the lifeboat could save the fourteen men who were waving from the rigging.

Bob Hook and other beachmen were meanwhile rescuing the master, his wife and three children, and the rest of the crew of the ketch *Q.E.D.*, of Dartmouth, which was ashore on the North Beach just about opposite the gasworks. Others were helping to save the crew of the schooner *Launceston*, of Fowey, and the schooner *Prosper*, of Caernarvon; a smackmaster, George Hall, won a silver medal from the RNLI for going out to the *Prosper* to the aid of a septuagenarian seaman who could not get ashore with the rest.

When the moon rose about half past nine watchers on the beach could see that the position of the men on the grounded colliers was desperate, and it was then that the visitors banged on Hook's door. Hook did go and unlock the doors of the lifeboat house, and, as was said at the inquiry that followed, he then did all he could to help launch the boat.

That was no easy matter, for the wreck of the *Q.E.D.* lay right opposite the lifeboat house, and the *Samuel Plimsoll* had to be hauled further along the beach before she could be launched. It all took time. While the lifeboat was being dragged out of her house the Coastguard arrived back from Pakefield and set about the job of sending a rocket line across the *Isis*. One man was hauled shorewards and was saved by one of the Coastguardsmen when, exhausted, he fell from the breeches buoy. It was at that point that the lifeboat arrived and took off seventeen men, the survivors of the *Isis*, the *Susanna Dixon* and the *Mornington*.

The Coastguards saved twenty-eight lives, and they were the heroes of that sad day. The lifeboat saved seventeen, and next morning went out to help bring in the billyboy ketch *Evening Star*, of Hull, which had been badly damaged in the gale.

A three-day public inquiry was held by the Lifeboat Institution, when a good head of steam was blown off, in the course of which reference was made to a deduction for two pints of beer for each man. It appeared that about 150 men put away this "lowance" on each occasion, according to some ancient rule of their forefathers, which caused some merriment, as also did the very pointed question addressed to one of the witnesses—"Who stole the bottle of whisky?" The only bright spots in a lamentable tale of woe. The inspector's report exonerated the committee from blame, with the exception of the hon. secretary and the superintendent, who were considered not to have carried out their duties properly. Bob Hook received the severest possible censure for gross and wilful neglect of duty; but the beachmen were not blamed, as they appeared to have had reasonable cause for dissatisfaction and were within their rights in acting as they did. They were told that their complaint would be considered by RNLI headquarters.

The two visitors were highly commended for their spirited exertions, which were the means of the lifeboat being launched in time to save some of those in peril.

It was said at the inquiry that there were then 119 members of the Old Company, ninety in the Young Company and about seventy in the North Roads Company, a total of nearly 300 beachmen. The Pakefield Beach Company had about seventy members as well. Times were becoming hard for these men, though, with the steam tugs taking over much of the work they had been accustomed to do and with other factors also acting against them.

They certainly had plenty to complain about. "We are allowed to go into danger for the good of others, and it may be to sacrifice our own lives," one beachman wrote in a letter to the newspaper in the aftermath of "Black Saturday," complaining that they were forbidden to use the lifeboat for salvage work, when they might prevent people imperilling their own lives, and were permitted to use it only when life was already in danger.

"Then we are brave fellows; but if we go out to vessels to prevent them getting into dangerous positions and obtain some remuneration for our services, then we are branded with the title of 'money grubbers' or 'longshore pirates.'"

It was in the *Samuel Plimsoll*, on 13th November, 1882, that Hook and his men rescued the crew of eight from the Norwegian barque *Berthon*. The lifeboat could hardly be seen between the huge seas, and it was thought at one time that she had been overwhelmed, but the crew succeeded in reaching the barque, which was being forced over the Holm Sand, and hauling her crew one by one into the lifeboat. It was a rescue, watched by thousands of people ashore, that helped to counter memories of "Black Saturday."

Of course there were many other gallant rescues in which Bob Hook

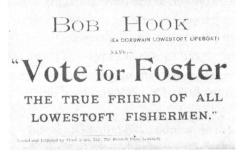

BOB HOOK
(Ex COXSWAIN LOWESTOFT LIFEBOAT)
SAYS:—

"Vote for Foster

THE TRUE FRIEND OF ALL
LOWESTOFT FISHERMEN."

Printed and Published by Flood & Son, Ltd. The Borough Press, Lowestoft.

Bob Hook in old age, wearing his medals, on an electioneering card.

played a notable part, kept in mind for many years by the old figureheads and nameboards decorating the Old Company's "shod" until it disappeared at the beginning of the Second World War. He seems to have given up the post of coxswain in 1883, when William "Spiley" Capps was appointed coxswain.

Unfortunately the RNLI headquarters has very few records of Hook's time as coxswain, but about 1907 there was published a short life of Bob Hook, taken down from the old hero himself, with the usual vagueness of those old boys as to names and dates. I acknowledge my indebtedness to the author.

I once saw Hook with Harry Foster, who was then fighting his last election in 1910. I remember that the old fellow was much distressed that his fraternity looked like turning down the "Fisherman's Friend."

Bob was then nearing harbour, and he finally finished life's voyage on 28th June, 1911. He lies in Lowestoft cemetery beneath a stone inscribed in these modest terms:

In ever-loving memory of this brave and noble man, Robert William Hook, who died June 28, 1911, aged 83 years. Thirty years coxswain of the Lowestoft lifeboat. Dearly-beloved husband of Sarah Ann Hook. His end was peace.

7 Jack Swan, King of the Longshoremen

JACK SWAN was born in 1857. He received the names of John Thompson Sterry Swan, and was surely entitled to the freedom of Lowestoft Beach, for were there not at one time three generations of Swans in the Old Company, while Sterrys are too well known in Lowestoft to need special mention.

It is therefore not surprising that at an early age he was taking a hand in the exciting and risky life of a yawlman, and came to be acknowledged as their best "timoneer" in the yawls *Success* and *Happy New Year*, and perhaps others I never knew. I sailed against him various times in the *Bittern*, and know he never gave anything away. In short, as a yawlman, Swan was "definitely hot stuff", as they say nowadays.

Naturally, as a longshoreman, he was always handy and soon became a member of the lifeboat crew. He was in the crew for fifty-two years, during which he took part in very many daring and arduous services. It is generally the spectacular or very successful services that the public hear of, but lifeboatmen go through many "rough do's" which never get further than the official service book, and the most easterly point of England is notorious for its dangerous ways when Davy Jones gets his shirt out; Jack Swan had more than his fair share of such services.

I never heard what part Swan played in the unhappy "Black Saturday" affair in 1882, but as it led to the establishment of a private lifeboat and Swan was coxswain of her for eight years I suspect he was well to the fore. That boat, the *Carolina Hamilton*, was built by Daniel Sparham in 1883 at a total cost of £450 and was named after the wife of Lord Claud Hamilton, who was for so long chairman of the Great Eastern Railway Company and was godfather to the Hamilton Dock.

I chiefly remember the *Carolina Hamilton* as a "bob-a-nob" boat at the South Pier steps in the holiday season, for about 1892 she was sold to Samuel Butcher, a pleasure boat proprietor, and I never heard that she did much lifeboat work. After the First World War I saw her as a houseboat at Wroxham, and as late as the 1950s she was still in Blake's list as a houseboat moored at Beccles.

If there was any estrangement it was put right and forgotten in after years, when, by dint of long and meritorious lifesaving work, Swan was chosen coxswain of the Institution boat in 1911. His time at the helm, of

The Lowestoft volunteer lifeboat *Carolina Hamilton* might not have had a great lifesaving record, but she was popular with holidaymakers who boarded her at the pier steps for trips into the Roads.

course, took in the whole of those anxious and troublous war years, when lifeboats were often called upon to take the great risk of floating mines and enemy action in addition to the usual perils of the sea. On 21st and 22nd November, 1914, he rescued the crews of the minesweepers *Spider* and *Condor*, two converted trawlers, aground on the Newcome Sand. For this service, carried out under circumstances of great difficulty, he was awarded the RNLI silver medal.

Then, on that wild night of 29th–30th September, 1918, I had him pulled out of bed at two in the morning when the *Pomona* was ashore south of Dunwich. The *Alfred Corry* at Southwold had been condemned and removed, and it was thought too bad for the small boat. I had tried Aldeburgh and Kessingland, but neither could do anything, and when I had explained the position to Swan he said they could not go either. Later, however, when I called up Lowestoft again and told him that the people were in the rigging and something must be done, he said he would try to get a crew.

Just after daylight I saw the Lowestoft boat tow past. With a crew of elderly men she crossed the shoal through heavy broken water and rescued nine poor devils who had been expecting to be washed away every minute of that stormy night. Their skipper had already been washed out of the rigging and drowned. Four of the men had to be dragged through the water by ropes.

For that splendid service the crew received extra pay from the RNLI, and Swan added a clasp to his silver medal.

We shan't forget the *Pomona* night. To give some idea of the work and worry which often fall upon lifeboat officials, without satisfactory result, I will set out my report of the case, which I stuck in my war diary:

> Was called at 2am winter time, by coastguard, who reported flares 1½ miles SE of Thorpe; met the Coxswain at the C.Gd. station. Blowing hard NE and raining. Rang up Aldeburgh and spoke to Coxswain; he said they could not go. Also spoke to Sizewell, Misner and the Sluice for information, then decided to muster for our small boat and fired gun about three. Proceeded to house, but only about a dozen men arrived. After waiting some time was informed they would not go in the small boat.
> Returned to C.Gd. station and spoke to Naval Base, being informed it was a Minesweeper ashore, an officer there authorized me to instruct Kessingland to launch, as we could not. Spoke to Coxswain of Kessingland boat, who said he could not get a crew. Reported this to Naval Base and Lowestoft C. Guards and spoke to Lowestoft Coxswain. After explaining circumstances to him he said he would try to get a crew. The wind meanwhile was turning off and at daybreak I decided to try again if we could get enough soldiers to drag the boat to the Harbour. Arranged this with an officer of the 17th Hants and at 5am fired the gun again and proceeded to house. After some time about eighteen men

turned up including five C. Guards, and when the soldiers came we got the boat out and dragged her to the Harbour. On arrival there found only six fishermen and the C. Guard had come down, and as I was told the other men would not go in the small boat, I gave it up and left the Rescue at the Ferry.

I returned to Coastguard station at 6.15 and saw the Lowestoft boat then passing and later was informed she had taken nine men out of the rigging.

Undoubtedly Swan's star performance was the rescue in October, 1922, of twenty-four men from the ss *Hopelyn* after they had been cooped up for nearly two days in the wireless cabin, with the hungry Scroby breakers raging all around. Coxswain William Fleming and the Gorleston crew in the pulling and sailing lifeboat *Kentwell* had earlier failed after the most determined efforts to get alongside the wreck, but Swan had the advantage of an engine, for the motor lifeboat *Agnes Cross* had been sent to Lowestoft the year before.

The story has been told before, sometimes in dramatic terms. Here is that great feat of the Lowestoft motor lifeboat, in the coxswain's own simple words.

> Called out Friday, October 20, at 4pm. to go to Gorleston to pick up Inspector Carver. We arrived at Gorleston 5pm, took Mr Carver on board, and proceeded towards the wreck. Before we got to her the Gorleston lifeboat *Kentwell* was coming away, so we spoke her, and took off the coxswain, and proceeded, but I got such a poor account of the wreck that I decided to wait till daylight, so we returned to Gorleston, left at 4am, and arrived at the wreck about six. Let go the anchor, wore down to her, took off the crew of twenty-four men and a black cat. The poor fellows had been in the Marconi house, 12 feet square, for thirty-six hours, with nothing to eat. The Gorleston lifeboat had tried to get to her two days but couldn't. Blowing a gale from ENE, we landed the crew at Yarmouth, and arrived home 8.15am. From the time we let go the anchor till we got the crew was ten minutes. Smart work!

Jack Swan makes the rescue sound simple, but it most certainly was not. The *Hopelyn* was breaking up, and the jagged edges of the broken plates were projecting outwards like huge knives. As the *Agnes Cross* approached the wreck she was picked up by an enormous sea and almost thrown on to

110

Coxswain Jack Swan, on the right, with Coxswain William Fleming of Gorleston holding a lifebuoy from the *Hopelyn* at the the time they were presented with their Gold Medals for the service to that ship.

the shattered after deck of the *Hopelyn*; "had it not been for the powerful motor fitted in this boat, I do not consider we could have got alongside," said Captain E.S. Carver, the Eastern District Inspector of Lifeboats, who was in the boat.

Even when the twenty-four men were aboard there were problems to be faced. The anchor cable had fouled part of the wreck, and it was impossible even to attempt to clear it. All that the coxswain could do was order the cable to be cut and put the engine full ahead to drag the boat clear. Just at that moment a terrific broadside sea submerged the lifeboat, threatening to wash the crew out of her.

The RNLI gold medals awarded to Jack Swan and to Coxswain Fleming were indeed well earned, and so were the silver medals awarded to Captain Carver and R. Scott, the motor mechanic of the *Agnes Cross*. Swan also received the OBE from the King himself at Buckingham Palace.

When a new lifeboat was being designed for Southwold, Jack Swan brought the Lowestoft boat to Southwold for the crew to see, and I then had the privilege of a ride in the *Agnes Cross* with the hero of the *Pomona* and *Hopelyn* rescues. Soon afterwards, in June, 1924, this veteran coxswain retired on pension after over half a century of lifeboat work during which he had helped to save 258 lives in Institution boats.

He never relaxed his interest in the service. He presented prizes, spoke at theatres and cinemas in London, and was heard on the wireless, always in support of the lifeboat, and his face was for many years seen representing the Suffolk coxswains in the Institution's appeals. For these services he was awarded the gold badge for honorary workers.

One of his last appearances was at the christening of the *Abdy Beauclerk* by Prince George at Aldeburgh on 27th May, 1932, when we sat side by side and talked of old friends and days long past. I only regret that distance prevented me from visiting him at Hopelyn Cottage and keeping in touch with a man whose friendship was a great privilege.

John Swan answered his last call on 20th February, 1935, at the ripe age of seventy-eight, but three of his sons followed his lead in lifeboat work, and his name and fame rest secure so long as lifeboats are talked of in Lowestoft.

"No county round the 5,000 miles of coastline of the British Isles has a finer record of gallantry in rescuing life from shipwreck than Suffolk," the Institution told me in 1937. "Its lifeboats have rescued no fewer than 2,850 lives."

To this I would add that up to that time seventy-nine medals for gallantry in saving life from shipwreck had been awarded by the Institution to Suffolk men, and well up on that roll of honour stand the names of these storm warriors from Lowestoft Beach.

8 Bygone Lifeboat Stations

IN THESE days of powerful motor lifeboats the number of stations in Suffolk has been reduced to three, at Lowestoft, Southwold and Aldeburgh, with Gorleston to the north and Harwich to the south.

Indeed, for some years Southwold was without a lifeboat after the *Mary Scott* was withdrawn in 1940 when a boom was put across the harbour to make it inaccessible to enemy invasion craft.

Gorleston used to be part of Suffolk, standing as it does on the Suffolk side of the Yare, but it is now a part of Norfolk, so I will only write a few notes on its earlier days when it was a Suffolk station. It has for some years now had modern motor lifeboats which can travel at speeds undreamed of by the old-timers who put to sea under sail.

The first lifeboat to be stationed at Gorleston was the unsuccessful North Country boat from Lowestoft, but it was not until 1866 that the RNLI established a station near the entrance to the harbour, sending the 33-foot self-righter *Leicester* there. There were lifeboats operated privately by the beach companies, however, craft of the Norfolk and Suffolk type built by local boatbuilders such as James Beeching, winner in 1851 of the Northumberland prize for the first self-righting design.

Thurston Hopkins, a Gorleston man, in his book *Small Sailing Craft* narrates the story of a great rescue on 15th February, 1855, of nine men from the mast of the brig *Anne Moore*, sunk on Corton Sand, by the Ranger Company's yawl *Breeze*. It was in that year that the lifeboat *Rescuer* was built by Beeching for the Ranger Company.

The *Rescuer* did some excellent salvage work and no doubt earned good money for the Ranger Company, but she proved an unlucky boat. She overturned one day in January, 1866, as she was going off and a dozen men were drowned, though four others were saved by another beach company lifeboat, the *Friend of All Nations*; one of the rescued men died later.

This disaster was responsible for the opening of the RNLI station at

Gorleston, for the Gorleston boatmen asked the Institution to send a surf boat because they believed such a boat, had it been available, might have saved some of the men lost from the *Rescuer*.

Nonetheless, the surf boat *Leicester* does not seem to have been effective when the *Rescuer*, repaired after the 1866 disaster, was involved in a more costly accident at the entrance to the harbour on 2nd December, 1867. She had picked up the crew of twenty-two of the full-rigged ship *George Kendall*, abandoned in the North Sea, and was returning when she came into collision with the lugger *James and Ellen*. Of the thirty-five men on board, twenty-five were drowned, the others being picked up by a boat which transferred them to the paddle tug *Andrew Woodhouse*.

It was a member of the Rangers, Edgar West Woods, known far and wide as "Laddie" Woods, who became coxswain of the *Leicester*. He had been in the *Rescuer* on 1st May, 1860, when she assisted to save the crew of seven of the *Ann* of Torquay, as well as the crew of a brig which had been in collision with the *Ann*, and he was one of those saved by the *Friend of All Nations* when the *Rescuer* overturned in 1866.

The Storm Company at Gorleston had the lifeboat *Refuge*, which was taken over by the Gorleston Voluntary Lifeboat Association when that body was formed in 1881. Under the ownership of the association the *Refuge* did some very good work, but when being towed back from a service by the paddle tug *United Service* on 10th November, 1888, she overturned with the loss of four of her crew. This disaster seems to have resulted from a misunderstanding between the lifeboat crew and the captain of the tug.

The overturning of the lifeboat and the subsequent rescue attempts in which four of the lifeboatmen were hauled from the sea by two Coastguards were watched by a small crowd on the pier, among whom was a Miss Elizabeth Simpson Stone, from Norwich. It was she who provided the money to build a replacement, named *Elizabeth Simpson* when launched from Beeching's yard on 23rd October the following year.

The *Elizabeth Simpson* did very good work over the next forty years and more. During a furious southerly gale on 13th October, 1891, the *Elizabeth Simpson* was launched in answer to torches burnt by the crew of the ketch *Ada*, of Portsmouth, which had struck on the Scroby. Owing to the direction and force of the wind and the sea on the bar a crew could not be got for her, but Woods and two pilots declared they were ready to make

114

The Gorleston volunteer lifeboat *Elizabeth Simpson*. Built at Beeching's yard in Gorleston, she was a donation from Miss Elizabeth Simpson Stone of Norwich.

the attempt. Following their lead, a full crew was obtained for the RNLI No 1 boat *Mark Lane*, a big Norfolk and Suffolk type boat which had been built by Beeching at almost the same time as the *Elizabeth Simpson*.

The *Mark Lane* was launched and tracked down the South Pier by a willing crowd. She only cleared the North Pier by a miracle and fine seamanship, and the shipwrecked crew were quickly rescued and landed at Gorleston. Then, the gale abating, the *Mark Lane* went out again and succeeded in salving the *Ada* as well. For this service "Laddie" received the silver medal and the two pilots votes of thanks from the RNLI. Altogether Woods was credited with assisting to save 443 lives, 172 of them in the RNLI boats.

The *Elizabeth Simpson* was fitted with two engines after the RNLI had sent a motor lifeboat, the *John and Mary Meiklam of Gladswood*, to Gorleston in 1924, and one of her finest rescues was carried out on 14th February, 1938, when she took seven people from the steam tanker *Tartary*, which had gone on the Haisborough Sand.

After the Second World War she became a pleasure trip boat at Yarmouth, and in extreme old age continued as a pleasure boat on the Broads.

At one time there were no fewer than four RNLI stations at Gorleston, which with the presence of the volunteer boat helps to account for the number of boathouses which used to line the riverside at Gorleston. A second boat was sent in 1883, and between 1892 and 1904 there was a third. The No 4 station was occupied by a steam lifeboat, first the *City of Glasgow*, transferred from Harwich for a six-month trial period in 1897, and then the *James Stevens No 3*, which was at Gorleston from 1903 to 1908.

In searching the various records of East Coast lifeboats I came across references to a station at Corton. This station was given a small Norfolk and Suffolk type boat built by Beeching in 1869 at a cost of £180, the entire cost of the station being borne by a Mrs. Davis, of Clapham, in memory of her husband; the boat was named the *Husband*. In the course of ten years the boat was launched only twice and saved three lives, so it is perhaps not surprising that the station closed in 1879 and the boat was transferred to Winterton as that station's No 2 boat. Gone is the beach from which the boat was launched and also the fishermen who used to work her, and still the insatiable ocean goes on devouring Corton, bite by bite.

The Pakefield station, one of the oldest in the county, was given a lifeboat built for the Suffolk Humane Society by William Teasdel at Yarmouth in 1840. This most useful Suffolk charity had been formed in 1806, and it continued to have sole control of the Lowestoft and Pakefield lifeboats until in 1855 it came to an arrangement with the RNLI whereby

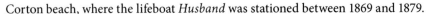

Corton beach, where the lifeboat *Husband* was stationed between 1869 and 1879.

116

that Institution would reward the crews while the Humane Society continued to pay the cost of supplying the boats. Indeed, it retained control of the two stations until 1873, when it handed them over lock, stock and barrel to the RNLI, though even then it did not hold its final meeting until 1892. From an old letter-book in my possession it is clear that the RNLI branch at Pakefield was not formed until 1889, when Mr. E.E. Johnson was appointed secretary and applied to Mr. B. Preston, the hon. secretary of the Lowestoft lifeboat, for the box and papers relating to the Pakefield boat.

There must have been many rescues there in the old days, but the earliest of which I have found any record is that on 26th January, 1842, of which I have written in chapter six. Those were the days of sailing coasters by the hundred who blundered through the old Fisherman's Gat, off Kessingland, or Pakefield Gat, now also closed, into or out of the South Roads and the little anchorage under the lee of the Ness, known for ages as Abraham's Bosom. Many were the wrecks there in blowing or foggy weather. Colman's *Lowestoft Handbook* (1860) tells of a violent north-east gale in the fifties when there were seven ships ashore in Pakefield Gat, and by repeated launches of the Pakefield boat every man jack of the crews was saved; a local gentleman sent the lifeboatmen £50 as a special reward.

That first boat served at Pakefield for thirty-two years; it was named *Sisters* in 1868, having apparently had no name until that time. In 1872 Daniel Sparham built a new boat, also named *Sisters* but renamed in 1876 *The Two Sisters, Mary and Hannah*, which was in service for no less than thirty-eight years. They built boats to last in those days.

A No 2 station was opened at Pakefield in 1871 with the *Henry Burford RN*, a small Norfolk and Suffolk type on a carriage, and this survived until 1895.

The first coxswain I know of was Nathaniel Colby, who took the Pakefield boat to the wreck of the *Zemira* in 1858, as I have told in chapter six. He won the silver medal for the rescue of the crew of the French schooner *La Jeune Mathilde* on the night of 31st October, 1859, after she had been driven on the beach opposite the Royal Hotel at Lowestoft. Coastguards using a mortar from the South Pier had managed to throw a line across the wreck, but the Frenchmen seemed to have no idea what to do with it, and they had to await the arrival of the Pakefield lifeboat. After considerable difficulty the Pakefield men managed to take off all the crew

The crew on the haul-off warp as the Pakefield lifeboat *The Two Sisters, Mary and Hannah* is launched from the beach.

except one, who obstinately refused to leave his ship. Eventually he had to be taken off by force.

At the inquiry at Lowestoft after the "Black Saturday" affair in 1882 evidence was given by George Meek Warford, coxswain of the Pakefield No 1 boat, and Nat Barber, coxswain of the No 2 boat. It appeared that the No 1 boat was launched after some delay, but that the No 2 boat could not be floated owing to the violence of the sea. George Warford I remember as a very capable and courageous coxswain; he earned the silver medal, with clasp for a second service, and retired about 1910. He was followed by John Ward, who was pensioned off when the Pakefield station closed in 1922 after many years of good work.

Once upon a time there was a longshore romance associated with Pakefield, where years ago the curate was the Reverend Swainson, brother of William Swainson, FRS, author of *Swainson's Birds* and a distinguished naturalist. With him lived his sister Elizabeth, well educated, romantic, and, probably owing to her Norse ancestry, deeply attached to the sea and those who followed it.

One day, when watching the return of the lifeboat, she saw a young, good-looking fisherman, James Peek by name, jump out of the boat. She fell in love with him on the spot. Perhaps not surprisingly there was family opposition to the match, but they made a runaway job of it and, so far as I know, lived happily ever after; but Mrs. Peek was a widow when I knew her. In P.H. Emerson's *Pictures of East Anglian Life* she tells her own story of their life together in the little macaroni schooner *Enterprise* and afterwards at Southwold, where she died about 1891, full of years and surrounded by cats. Her only son, Gabriel Peek, was also a lifeboatman and, like his grandfather, Robert Peek, of Southwold, was drowned while fishing in Solebay, a year or two after his mother's death.

Kessingland is next of the closed stations on our bit of coast. The Southwold lifeboat *Solebay* was sold to the Kessingland beachmen in 1855, and apparently continued to serve there as a beachmen's lifeboat until 1869, though there is no record of her work. The Institution opened a station there in 1867, when the *Grace and Lally of Broadoak*, a 32-foot Norfolk and Suffolk type built by Beeching in that year, was sent to Kessingland to work alongside the beachmen's *Solebay*. In 1870 a second, larger boat also built by Beeching, the *Bolton*, joined her, apparently replacing the beachmen's lifeboat. The smaller boat was kept about two

Launching the Pakefield lifeboat *James Leath*, which was built by Thames Iron Works at Milwall in 1910.

119

miles south of Kessingland to be opposite the most dangerous part of the Barnard Sand and the Covehithe Channel, where vessels often came to grief in those days. She was known locally as the Benacre boat, but was manned from Kessingland.

Renamed *St. Michael's, Paddington* in 1879, the smaller boat was replaced in 1897 by a new boat also from Beeching's yard, the *St. Paul*, which was transferred to the No 1 station when the Benacre or No 2 station was closed in 1918. On the closure I bought one of the boathouses and had it removed to Southwold harbour, where it stood on the quay, a tribute to the good, solid work and stuff put into those places before corrugated iron and the George V style came to defile the countryside. For a few years between 1884 and 1896 there was even a No 3 station at Kessingland with the *Charles Bury*, a 38-foot Norfolk and Suffolk, but she launched on service only twice and saved no lives on either occasion.

Most celebrated of the Kessingland coxswains was George Strowger, known as "Gaffer", who was voted the silver medal in 1883 "in recognition of his gallant services in those boats since the establishment of the station". He was awarded a second service clasp when he retired in 1895, to be succeeded as coxswain by George Roth and then, five years later, by his nephew, Robert "Young Gaffer" Strowger.

A beach yawl on Kessingland beach dressed for the local regatta in the early years of the 20th century.

With the advent of motor boats at Lowestoft and Southwold there was less need for a lifeboat at Kessingland, and the station was closed in 1937, when the last boat, the *Hugh Taylor*, was removed.

The station at Southwold was closed a few years later when Southwold harbour was closed and the motor lifeboat *Mary Scott*, just back from Dunkirk, was transferred to the RNLI's reserve fleet. For more than twenty years there was no lifeboat in the harbour, and then in 1963 an inshore rescue boat was sent. A whole new chapter was beginning.

A few miles south of Southwold harbour is the village of Dunwich, once a thriving port and trading community until the sea destroyed it. A lifeboat was sent to Dunwich in 1873 in answer to the application of the vicar of Dunwich, the Reverend John Frederick Noott, who became the first hon. secretary.

The minute book, found among the town records after they had been taken to the Suffolk Record Office, provides a fascinating insight into the organisation of a lifeboat station in Victorian times. While Mr. Noott saw to the day-to-day running of the

A painting of the Dunwich lifeboat in its house at the time the Reverend John Frederick Noott was hon. secretary. The site of the boathouse is now under the sea.

establishment a leading role was taken by the patron, who was the local squire, Frederick Barne, and the president, his brother Lieut.-Col. St. John Barne. On occasion the minutes record "proposed by the Squire, seconded by the Colonel. . .".

A 30-foot self-righting lifeboat was put in hand by T. & W. Forrestt at Limehouse after the RNLI committee of management had decided in March to establish the station, but when the United States Life Saving Service asked for advice on a design for use on the American coast the RNLI arranged for them to buy this boat, which underwent self-righting trials on 21st July. Dunwich had to wait until October for Forrestt to

121

complete another boat, which was christened *John Keble* after the author of *The Christian Year*, whose family defrayed the cost of the boat.

As a very small but interested nipper I saw her drawn by horses to the church for a dedication service on 9th October, 1873, and afterwards witnessed the actual christening and launch, being intensely thrilled to see one of the crew jump overboard as she was returning and swim ashore in his cork jacket.

Six months after the opening of the station the committee were investigating "the circumstances attending the wreck of the *Alma* on Sizewell Bank and the reasons why the Dunwich Boat *The John Keble* did not proceed to the wreck to assist the Thorpe Boat". The lifeboat *Ipswich* had gone out from Thorpe and rescued three of the crew, but had been unable to get the rest, and it was left to the much bigger Southwold No 1 boat to take off the remaining crew members early next morning. The committee was soon being told quite sharply by the RNLI secretary in London that "the Dunwich Life Boat was never intended for work on the Sizewell Bank, inasmuch as that came within the province of the Southwold and Thorpe boats, and that therefore you were perfectly justified, even tho' you had seen the vessel on the Bank, not to send your Boat off to her".

That winter the lifeboat inspector "expressed himself as perfectly satisfied with the proficiency of the crew and the state of the Boat and all the gear," but recommended that the roadway to Minsmere should be widened so that the lifeboat could be taken along it if the need arose. In 1876 the lifeboat was indeed taken overland to Sizewell when the Danish brig *Peter* struck on the outer shoal abreast of the Coastguard station at Minsmere.

Again the committee held an inquiry as to why the coxswain had decided to take the boat by road rather than launching at Dunwich and sailing to windward to reach the wreck. The Coastguards were strongly of the opinion that the crew had been wrong in what they did, and some of the committee members wanted a fresh crew and a new coxswain. Eventually they decided to call in the Inspector of Lifeboats.

The Inspector, Admiral Robertson-Macdonald, came down heavily on the side of Coxswain Edward Brown, saying that if he had been present he would have ordered the boat to be taken to Sizewell overland and have launched her there. Furthermore, he said, it was of great importance for the crew and the Coastguard to work together in harmony, and without rivalry.

In spite of the admiral's support for him the coxswain was sacked the following year, "in consequence of his continued practice of using abusive language". He insisted on appealing to the president and the chairman of the local branch, but Squire and Colonel were adamant.

Eventually the rumpus subsided and it was "proposed by the Squire, seconded by the Colonel, that the Deputy Coxswain, Isaac Dix, be appointed Coxswain. . ." Thus Isaac Dix began his eighteen years as coxswain.

Dix was in charge of the *John Keble* on the only occasion she was launched on service, on 27th December, 1886, when she saved the mate of the *Day Star*, of Ipswich, on Thorpe Ness. The Southwold lifeboat *The London Coal Exchange* saved four more men from the vessel, but the cook, John Catchpole, was lost. At the same time seven men were saved by the Thorpe rocket apparatus from the brig *Trixie Wee*.

After fourteen years the *John Keble* was replaced in 1887 by the rather larger *Ann Ferguson*, which was seven years on the station, was launched five times and saved twenty lives. Her star service was the rescue of fourteen from the barque *Flora* of Öland, sunk on Sizewell Bank on 3rd November, 1888. The wind was strong at east-south-east and the sea heavy; one of the crew was washed overboard but was recovered with nothing worse than a ducking, and Isaac Dix beached the boat at Sizewell, from where the shipwrecked crew were taken to the Vulcan Arms, "a public house of the old-fashioned kind, with low rooms more comfortable than commodious," to quote a contemporary report.

In 1894 the *Lily Bird* was exchanged for the *Ann Ferguson*, which was taken to Darsham station to be sent back to London by rail. In those days the Great Eastern Railway usually carried lifeboats to the nearest station free of charge.

Mr. Noott died towards the end of 1894 and Edward Lingwood, an artist who had moved from Ipswich to The Ferns, Dunwich, a year or two before, took over as secretary. He had problems in picking up the reins of office, and when a committee meeting was held at his home he reported that "there were no minutes to read; there did not appear to have been a committee meeting for the last 10 years. . ."

One of the men summoned to that meeting sent a letter in which he said "How my name got on the committee I do not know. I was never asked to serve nor have I ever been summoned to a meeting. I can only suppose that the late Mr. Noott wanted a committee man and so put my name on the list. He did such sort of things sometimes."

There were other problems, for Dix had been injured at a launch the previous year, and at the age of sixty-four he felt he could not carry on as coxswain. The crew chose a new coxswain who did not meet with the approval of the committee members, and the reason became obvious when at a later meeting the secretary reported that the new coxswain had called at his home on Christmas Eve in a state of intoxication. The result was that he was replaced as coxswain, having held the post for less than two months.

To these problems were added difficulties in finding sufficient fishermen to man the boat, even when sanction was given for some of the Minsmere Coastguards to join the crew. In 1903 the decision was taken to close the Dunwich station, and the RNLI decided to compensate for the closure by placing a second lifeboat on Aldeburgh beach; in 1905 a new Liverpool type boat, the *Edward Z. Dresden*, took up her duties there alongside the No 1 boat, the *City of Winchester*. Dunwich lifeboat house has been long washed away and there are neither Coastguards nor fishermen there today.

The story of some of the earliest lifeboats on the Suffolk coast is bound up with the history of the Suffolk Association for Saving the Lives of Shipwrecked Seamen, founded at a meeting attended by the High Sheriff of the county and other important and noble residents of Suffolk at the Shire Hall in Bury St. Edmunds on 16th October, 1824. It was only the second county lifesaving association in the country; the first had been established the year before in Norfolk.

The Duke of Grafton was in the chair at the inaugural meeting and adjourned to 8th November at Stowmarket King's Head, when it was resolved to support those lifeboats already in existence on the coast. The association voted £20 each to Landguard, Bawdsey and Lowestoft, as well as £35 to put the Landguard boat in repair, and arranged to meet twice a year at Ipswich and Bury. Sub-committees were appointed for the three districts, to meet at Ipswich, Aldeburgh and Lowestoft, though the Suffolk Humane Society continued to have complete responsibility for the boat at the latter place.

Before the end of the year the "Committee of Controul" of the Suffolk Shipwreck Association, as it became popularly known, decided to spend not more than £200 on building a lifeboat to be stationed at Orford and to place a number of lifesaving mortars at selected places on the coast. The new boat was built by William Plenty at his boatyard up the River Kennett at Newbury, an unlikely place for the birth of such a craft. She was of the type designed by Plenty some years earlier but of an "improved model", 24 feet long and 8 feet in the beam, pulling eight oars.

It took until March, 1826, for her to arrive at her station, but she cost only £168 against the £200 the association had budgeted, and the decision was promptly taken to purchase a similar boat for Sizewell Gap. The Orford boat was named *Grafton*, after the association's president, the Duke of Grafton.

Unfortunately few records appear to exist of the Suffolk Shipwreck Association, and nothing is known of the work of the Orford boat. She was manned from the town of Orford but kept on Orfordness, in a shed not far from the two lighthouses there. The

This print of the Orfordness lighthouses published by John Murray in 1838 shows the Orford lifeboat approaching a wrecked brig to take off the crew. Nothing is known of this rescue, if indeed it took place.

Sizewell boat is recorded as rescuing the crew of the sloop *Catherina*, of Goole, one day in 1841. Later she went out again and, helped by a boat from Thorpe, took the dismasted sloop into Yarmouth, so no doubt the crew claimed their share of salvage.

Two years after taking over from the Suffolk Association for Saving the Lives of Shipwrecked Seamen, the RNLI in 1853 sent the *Grafton*, which during the 1830s had been transferred from Orfordness to Woodbridge Haven, to Thorpe to open a new station there. The whole of the period during which Thorpe had a lifeboat is covered by the ninety-year-long life of William Alexander, who became coxswain of the first *Ipswich* after

Joshua Chard, whose story is told in chapter one.

The *Grafton* spent two years at Thorpe before being replaced by an unnamed 30-foot self-righter built by Beeching in 1852 and repaired by Forrestt in 1854-55. She had spent her first couple of years at Boulmer, in Northumberland. She did good service in 1855, and again during the winter of 1859-60 and the following year.

In 1862 her place was taken by the first *Ipswich*, a self-righter built by Forrestt and paid for by subscriptions raised in Ipswich. She was launched into the Orwell on 29th May, 1862, in the presence of 5,000 people. Eight years later this boat was replaced by a second *Ipswich*, formerly the Gorleston lifeboat *Leicester*, which was transferred to Skegness after only

The launching at Ipswich of the first lifeboat named *Ipswich* on 29th May, 1862. Paid for by a subscription paid for in the town, she was stationed at Thorpe and served there for only eight years before being replaced by another boat given the same name.

three years on Thorpe beach and replaced by yet another *Ipswich*, a larger self-righter again built by Forrestt at Limehouse.

In April, 1871, the Thorpe boat lay all night by the barque *Alma* on Sizewell Bank. At daylight the Southwold boat arrived and took out fourteen hands, Alexander in the Thorpe boat having already saved three, and both boats ran for Aldeburgh beach.

When Alexander at last retired he was followed by his son Alfred, who carried on the family traditions and was coxswain of the last Thorpe boat, the *Christopher North Graham*. The Thorpeness station closed in 1900, having been credited with the saving of 93 lives during almost half a century.

The Thorpe lifeboat *Ipswich*, second of that name, photographed on Thorpe beach.

Old Alexander died in January, 1913, at the age of ninety and his boy was cut off in 1936 at the age of seventy-seven. With him, I expect, passed the last of the old-time Thorpemen.

The Sizewell boat that had been built for the Suffolk Shipwreck Association in 1826 remained there for 25 years and was then transferred to Aldeburgh, which station was given a new self-righting boat in 1853. The new boat was at Aldeburgh for seventeen years, was lengthened by Forrestt from 32 feet to 39 feet in 1860 after she had capsized with the loss of three of her crew, and was given the name *Pasco* in 1866.

More of the story of this station, which is still in existence, is to be found in chapter four.

At Bawdsey was one of the two earliest Suffolk lifeboats, built by Henry Greathead in 1801 at the same time that he was building another for Lowestoft. The *Ipswich Journal* of 18th February, 1804, reported that she had just had a successful trial and had saved the crew of a collier brig, the *Pallas*, of London, which had struck the bank in the early morning and sunk. The lifeboat failed to reach the vessel at the first attempt as the crew was composed in part at least of inexperienced hands, but when another crew of experienced seamen took over they saved seven men and a woman from the rigging, in which they had spent nearly six terrible hours.

The same boat was out again in 1808, when it was hauled nearly two miles by a team of horses and was launched about midnight in the vicinity of Woodbridge Haven to go to the aid of a brig making signals of distress near the Cutler Sand. Perhaps the crew were landsmen again, because they seem to have allowed the boat to fill through the plughole and had to put back, leaving it for some smacksmen to bring the leaking brig into the Deben.

This boat was known locally as the Hollesley Bay lifeboat, for the *Suffolk Chronicle* of 3rd August, 1811, reports a meeting of Hollesley Bay lifeboat subscribers at Bawdsey Star, when it was resolved that a committee of management should be appointed to look after the boat and house at Bawdsey, and a large sum was raised by subscription. The *Ipswich Journal* of 20th November, 1824, reports a meeting of that committee at Bawdsey Star on 11th November, with Vice-Admiral Carthew in the chair, when they inspected the boat and saw her exercised with great satisfaction.

The Bawdsey boat was moved to Woodbridge Haven in 1825, the boathouse being re-erected on the point below where Bawdsey Manor was later built by Sir Cuthbert Quilter. There is no record of any work done while she was there, and at some time in the 1830s her place was taken by the *Grafton*, which was transferred from Orford. The station seems to have been closed in 1853 when the *Grafton* was moved to Thorpe.

An interesting lifeboat was built by Jabez Bayley at Ipswich in 1821 from a design by Captain Richard Hall Gower, a former East India officer whose pastime seems to have been producing vessels of revolutionary design. This boat was thirty-one feet long by only six feet beam, double ended and rigged with two very short masts carrying spritsails. To give her buoyancy she had eleven cubic feet of cork and fifty cubic feet of copper air-cases, and she was fitted with two self-delivery tubes by which she could be cleared of water.

A great crowd watched her launching from Jabez Bayley's yard just below Stoke Bridge on 4th April, 1821, after which she was tested in the Orwell with twenty-five men on board, in addition to her own crew of seven.

The subscription to pay for the building of this boat was raised by Admiral Benjamin Page, an Ipswich-born naval officer who had spent much of his service in Indian waters at a time when Britain and France were engaged in a struggle for supremacy in the East. He had gone out to India first when he joined the *Superb* at the age of thirteen; by the time he was eighteen he had fought in four fleet actions, in one of which he was severely wounded in the leg.

This lifeboat was stationed at Landguard Fort, under the superintendence of the lieutenant-governor of the fort, and was to be used by crews of vessels in Harwich to save life or assist any craft getting into difficulties when making that port.

She was launched on the night of 19th February, 1824, to the brig *Elvina*, ashore on the Platters with her rudder gone, and helped to get her off and into harbour. She was manned on that occasion by six coastguards under Coxswain Harvey, and a subscription was raised for them.

The Suffolk Shipwreck Association voted £35 to put her in repair when it met on 8th November, 1824, and on 18th December that year it was reported that she had been repaired and returned to her station, having been much improved by adding 2ft 6in to her breadth.

The expenditure does not seem to have had much beneficial effect, for in October the following year the Shipwreck Association appointed a committee to investigate the suitability of Landguard Fort as a lifeboat station, and it reported that it was "of no use whatever". The boat herself was said to be "totally inefficient".

By March, 1827, she had been converted to a yacht and was for sale at the shipyard in Ipswich from which she had been launched with such high hopes only six years before. In the 1840s the Admiralty stationed a lifeboat, built by Thompson, of Rotherhithe, at Landguard, but she did not do very much work in the few years she was there.

It would be pleasant to know more of the bygone lifeboat stations of this wild and stormy coast, but the early records have almost all been lost and it is only in the files of old newspapers that one can sometimes find a tantalising reference to long-forgotten lifeboats, bygone stations and courageous old seadogs.

Index

135

Lightning Source UK Ltd.
Milton Keynes UK
UKOW03f2247190713

214085UK00001B/12/P